Children's
Literature Gems

Choosing and Using Them in
Your Library Career

Elizabeth Bird

AMERICAN LIBRARY ASSOCIATION
CHICAGO 2009

Elizabeth Bird is a senior children's librarian with New York Public Library's Children's Center at 42nd Street. She runs the children's literary blog *A Fuse #8 Production* on the *School Library Journal* website. She has written articles for *Horn Book Magazine* and currently reviews for *Kirkus*. In 2004 she earned her master's degree in library and information science at the College of St. Catherine in St. Paul, Minnesota.

The paper used in this publication meets the minimum requirements of American National Standard for Information Sciences—Permanence of Paper for Printed Library Materials, ANSI Z39.48-1992. ∞

Library of Congress Cataloging-in-Publication Data
Bird, Elizabeth, 1978–
    Children's literature gems : choosing and using them in your library career / Elizabeth Bird.
        p. cm.
    Includes bibliographical references and index.
    ISBN 978-0-8389-0995-9 (alk. paper)
    1. Children's libraries—Book selection. 2. Children—Books and reading—United States. 3. Children's literature—Bibliography—Methodology. 4. Children's librarians—United States.   I. Title.
    Z718.2.U6B57 2009
    027.62'5—dc22

                                                                        2009003079

ISBN-13: 978-0-8389-0995-9

Printed in the United States of America
13 12 11 10 09   5 4 3 2 1

Children's
Literature Gems

Contents

Introduction

In my career as a children's librarian in New York City, I have often felt that I was hit over the head with the lucky stick (so to speak). My first job was in a Greenwich Village branch, the Jefferson Market Library, as the head of the children's room. After a year working with young readers on the Lower West Side, I was given the chance to fill a vacancy in New York Public Library's Central Children's Room, now known as the Children's Center at 42nd Street. Working in that environment gave me a chance to delve into old texts, historical files, and a massive collection. One of the greatest perks, however, was being in a library considered a destination by children's librarians from all over the country. From my vantage point at the reference desk, I could meet people from the world over and ask them about their own library systems when they walked in to admire my own. I've had the opportunity to learn a lot from these encounters, to say nothing of my discussions with other professionals during library and book conferences. Without question, librarians who work with young people are some of the fittest, most intelligent, downright fun individuals you can meet. Even more remarkable is the amount of spare time they dedicate to their profession. After all, recommendations and collection development are at the heart of the job, but certain questions come up. How does your average everyday librarian find such books? What award winners should you, the librarian, know about, and how do you recommend books that have received awards to people who have never heard of them? What is the difference between an award winner and a classic?

Talk to any library professional who deals with small fry on a regular basis, and the motto of almost every children's librarian could well be, "No rest for the weary." Children's librarianship is a profession that requires a constant commitment to keeping up-to-date on changes in the field. My own spare time is filled with reading children's books: on the subway, on car trips, in bed, on the couch, in the air, during bad movies, you name it. And many other librarians in the field choose to fill their off-hours with children's literature in one form or another.

Mind you, periodically you will hear professional critics decry the infantilization of our culture. When the world waited to read the newest Harry Potter book, reviewers like novelist and poet A. S. Byatt lamented the existence of the "childish adult" who could take pleasure in such literature. Nevertheless, we children's librarians are unabashed in our out-and-out love of books for children. And most of us do not give up our own pleasure in reading adult literature for the sake of keeping up-to-date with children's books. We know how to distinguish between the two. That doesn't mean that reading books for children isn't fun, though! The ability to enjoy this job to the fullest is one of the requirements of the field. Those with only a passing interest in the bread and butter of the occupation may be in trouble. After all, it's hard to promote something on a regular basis if you don't get a kick out of it yourself.

People are considered fortunate if they find themselves in a profession that makes them feel good, and many supplement their working hours by taking pleasure in professional development. I run a children's literary blog and a children's literary podcast, belong to the child_lit electronic mailing list, visit library conferences, and review for professional publications like *Kirkus*. Children's literature is one of the most rewarding fields to be in, and public librarianship is the natural place to apply what you have learned along the way. So when I fill my time with these side ventures, I tend to have a blast. And I'd love to give other people the tools for having as much professional fun as I do.

This book is for public children's librarians and up-and-coming members of the field who would like to round out their knowledge and embrace all of children's literature. We all need to stretch out of our comfort zone once in a while, becoming the fully informed individuals the world expects us to be. One of the best jobs a librarian has is instilling a lifelong love of learning in children, and selecting great children's books is just one of many parts of our jobs. As librarian Harriet Long once said, we need "to encourage lifelong education . . . to help the child develop to the full his personal ability and social understanding, and to serve as a social force in the community together with other agencies concerned with the child's welfare" (Rollock 1988, 8). That said, this book concerns itself primarily with helping you, the public children's librarian, acquire a rounded knowledge of the titles out there, old and new, well known and obscure. I look at that notion of children's library materials of "quality" and how we come to terms with including great literature alongside schlock. I also offer ideas on how to work your knowledge of great books into your everyday librarian duties. There will be hints of what you can do in your spare time, if you'd like to supplement your love of the job in your off-hours. Basically, consider this book a collection of tips on how to wholly immerse yourself in all aspects of children's librarianship.

I know that in my own case, there is always a temptation to coast on whatever knowledge of children's books I've retained since my youth. For example, if a ten-year-old comes up to me and asks for something scary, my first instinct is to grab *Scary Stories to Tell in the Dark* by Alvin Schwartz (1981) or *Wait Till Helen Comes* by Mary Downing

Why are you a children's librarian?

I am "old school." I became a children's librarian because I love books and reading, love recreation with youth (like programming and arts and crafts), and did lots of community theater, so storytime came naturally for me. I also like research and "homework," and it was my college advisor who recommended library school to me, instead of teaching, based on my hobbies, and the fact I was an American history major. My MLS thesis is on film, and the media collection is another part of my job (not just children's DVDs but for adults too), which I really enjoy, so this job was the perfect fit. I often tell other librarians the best experience for this job was when I was the manager of a restaurant-nightclub, since I had to host entertainment shows, serve customers, deal with money, do time sheets and schedules, *and* kick out rowdy people, all of which I still do as a children's librarian!

Penny Peck, senior librarian, Branch Services,
San Leandro Public Library, California

Hahn (1986). These instincts aren't wrong (particularly since both books are still in print), but you need to supplement them with more contemporary fare. If you were a voracious reader as a child, then certainly you may have a leg up in this occupation. But what you learn in the present is just as important as what you retain from your past. If we don't keep up-to-date, we'll quickly find that the children entering our libraries are essentially speaking a foreign language. Sometimes when I am at a reference desk and a child asks at lightning speed whether we have the latest fairy/TV show/series title, what they see on my part is a blank face and guppylike mouthing as I try to translate exactly what it is they're looking for. It's good to know what's popular, even if you merely familiarize yourself with current literature with the sole intent of redirecting your patrons to the classics you prefer ("You want Junie B. Jones? Say, have you ever read Ramona?").

Of course, you are only one person. You can't read everything. You are also not five or ten or thirteen years old, so falling behind the times seems inevitable. How are you supposed to know what the hot new titles are or, for that matter, how best to promote them? Maybe your library system is so slow you won't even see the top-selling books until weeks or months after they've been released. It's easy to feel reluctant to stretch yourself and delve deeper into a profession you already know so well. But the result is that kids asking for the latest title in their favorite series or on a contemporary subject are sometimes met with a soul-crushing blank stare—the stare that says that their favorite librarian neither knows nor cares about a subject near and dear to their hearts.

For some of us, keeping up with the new is easy. These librarians are perfectly comfortable with the newest books published, but they may not have had a chance to delve deep into the classics and older award-winning works of children's literature. They're happy to peruse the newest titles coming out on the market today, but ask them to recommend their top ten Newbery winners prior to 1980, and problems arise. On the surface, a knowledge of older books might seem necessary only for librarians who run book clubs or write recommended lists of titles. This is not necessarily the case. If we assume that a librarian's job consists of critiquing new titles, how can you justify doing that without comparing and contrasting them to the old? If you'd never read an Anne McCaffrey book about the dragon riders of Pern, can you fairly assess *Eragon,* a story about a boy and his dragon? What if someone comes in looking for your favorite version of the story of *Tam Lin*? Are you able to compare the different versions, new and old, and assess which one is the best? Librarians with small budgets know all too well that when it comes to building a collection, you need to know and make use of the books you already have, in addition to the titles you're buying.

So let's say that there are two different kinds of librarians out there: the Historian and the Up-to-Date Specialist. The one is a true expert on the past, the other a sterling promoter of the present. Mind you, most experienced librarians read the newest titles voraciously, just as people fresh out of library school often make a point to read through a wide variety of old best-book lists. The length of your term in the profession does not indicate whether you are a Historian or an Up-to-Date Specialist at heart. In this book, we'll look at the exact nature of the children's librarian job, considering such factors as where we came from and where we are today. We'll get to know how and why the children's librarians of the past located materials and judged them worthy of inclusion in their collections. We'll consider how that has changed today and look at the current state of books and their large and small publishers. We'll also look at moving beyond the award winners to scout out the best contemporary books and popular titles.

Knowing the books is only half the battle, though. It's using the books in a constructive fashion that really gives them the attention they so richly deserve. How do you find the best preschool books

And how did you come to this profession?

I kind of fell into children's librarianship. It was what I really wanted to do, but it wasn't heavily promoted when I was in library school at the University of Minnesota years ago (I took the one class there was), and there weren't any children's positions available in the Twin Cities area when I got my degree. As luck would have it, my then-boyfriend-now-husband moved to San Francisco for a postdoc position, and they needed children's librarians. They danced with joy when I applied at the San Francisco Public Library and said I'd love to work as a children's librarian. My best qualification was I knew a lot of children's books, because I always loved them best and never stopped reading them. I'd never worked with kids before—I barely knew any kids at that time—but I had a sneaking suspicion that if I enthusiastically shared a book that I loved with kids, they might like it too. I was right. It didn't hurt that I kind of like to perform in front of an audience.

Carla Kozak, development specialist, Children and Youth Services,
San Francisco Public Library

without turning each storytime into a testing zone? What makes a great read-aloud to a class of bored second graders? And when it comes to booktalks, how do you pluck the scintillating marrow from a gripping tale of nonfiction and make kids want to read it?

Your precious free time when you are not in a library setting is yours to do with as you please. Should you feel obligated to supplement your job with professional development during your off-hours? How do your daily life, trends, family, and other variables affect you, and what can you take from home that will work in the library itself? Is reviewing right for you? And are you the kind of person who would enjoy blogging, or is that not something you're interested in?

This book is dotted and speckled with a variety of best-book listings that cover everything from the best books in children's literature to picture books that read aloud beautifully to large groups. Creating lists for your patrons is an important and too little lauded skill. Often I'll be seated at the reference desk, and a patron will ask for a list of recommended picture books, princess stories, Cinderella tales from around the world, or just fun middle-reader chapter books. Having lists handy and available can make your job easier. The lists in this book reflect my own preferences and picks, and I encourage you to make your own.

What got you into children's librarianship?

When I came as Walter the Giant Storyteller to the Girls' Middle School in October 2001, I came to tell stories and enthuse about books at this place where my friend Ann Woodrow worked. Ann was having an annus horribilis, and the school was looking for someone to take over the program she had started. In essence, I was the storyteller who never left. I thought myself unsuited for working in the same place with the same people every day. I hadn't done it in years! But I find that as with so many other things in my life, if I jump, the universe catches me. I jumped and landed here and have found a home beyond my wildest imaginings. I get to spend my days ministering to the needs of 140 sixth-, seventh-, and eighth-grade girls who enrich my life beyond measure, and it turns out, I have quite the aptitude for middle school.

Or as one of my former students says: "Walter, you're so good with middle school girls because you *are* a middle school girl!"

Walter M. Mayes, author, storyteller, and book maven; librarian,
Girls' Middle School, Mountain View, California

If you believe that it's a crime against humanity that Kate DiCamillo's fiction title *The Miraculous Journey of Edward Tulane* is not included on my best fiction listing, that can encourage you to make your own list—one that will truly speak to your own community.

The public perception that children's librarians just sit around all day and read kids' books may be a mistaken notion, but it does hint at one thing correctly. Our job is, not to put too fine a point on it, awesome. Just ask the hundreds of parents and teachers who walk through your doors every day with a wistful gleam in their eye and a stirring desire to join the field. For me, children's librarianship is my job as well as my hobby. It doesn't have to be that way for you, of course. I'm not asking you to implement all the ideas I've listed here, but instead incorporate the ones that work for you. This book will allow you to pick up some tips for finding and using children's literature in your everyday activities, both at work and at home. Whether librarianship is as comfortable to you as a pair of old gloves or a new and exciting field into which you've just arrived, let this book be your guide in finding, using, and appreciating the bulk of children's books out there.

No single librarian has all the answers. Consequently I've asked some of the best children's librarians in the field to contribute their thoughts to my different questions pertaining to the field. From their responses, scattered in the boxes throughout this book, you will find an array of expertise and talents touching on almost every aspect of children's librarianship. A big thank-you to all the contributors for taking the time to share their knowledge.

ONE

History

or, Why We Willingly Remain under Ranganathan's Thumb

You are part of one of the noblest professions in the world! True, you don't heal the sick, but just look at the sheer amount of good that an average children's literary professional does every day. If literature aids in furthering human knowledge and understanding, then encouraging children to read is one of the building blocks of our civilization.

In the past, children's librarians had to justify their very existence to the world. It's funny to consider it today, but people used to question whether children even belonged in a library setting. Now, nobody questions the importance of having children in the libraries, but some people (school boards and city governments, for example) do wonder how necessary it is for *librarians* to be there in the face of new technological wonders in the library.

Looking back through history, we should take note of where children's librarians came from and how they located materials for their young patrons, particularly when the demand for books outweighed the amount of product.

NINETEENTH CENTURY: CHILDREN? IN LIBRARIES? GADZOOKS!

We've come a long way since the days when a children's librarian was merely "expected to have a thorough knowledge of these titles in order to guide the child's reading intelligently" (Rollock 1988, 6). We're still hoping to do that, of course, but our duties and skills have expanded immeasurably. Now we're expected to be singing, hand-rhyming performers who also know our materials, both past and present.

The idea of keeping up with the newest children's books was rather a moot point before the 1800s. Early American libraries weren't too keen on the notion of providing children with good reading material. (Actually they weren't too keen on the notion of having children in the library, period.) The early nineteenth century was primarily a time when libraries were seen as a guiding influence over the newest crop of immigrants. And what better way to assimilate these arrivals than through the public library system? Oddly enough, the notion of extending that same courtesy to their children didn't come up until around 1876, when author William I. Fletcher argued that if children didn't become good readers early on, they'd develop a taste for dime novels and other tawdry reading material. And with the average child attaining a mere five years of education, librarians decided that they were the best hope for promoting lifelong reading habits in their young charges (Tyack 1978).

The idea to grant children use of the library began to gain some ground in the late nineteenth century. It was tied into the broader movement to pay more attention to children at the time. The progressive movement was promoting various social welfare reforms, and librarianship was due for an overhaul. After all, during the late nineteenth century, the newly created children's librarian's charge was the moral, spiritual, and cultural well-being of young clientele. The better the books, the better the child, and "librarians, for their part, were convinced that children who were exposed to fine, uplifting literature would grow up to be fine, uplifted adults" (Walter 2001, 2). Therefore, everything chosen by these library professionals was meant to meet three standards: literary quality, child appeal, and good values.

The problem? Putting librarians in charge of children generated an entirely new criticism. There was now a great deal of controversy surrounding the "feminization of the library" (Hunt 1917) due to the sheer number of women versus men working in the field. Putting women in charge of something as important as choosing the books a young person could read meant to some minds that they might purchase primarily flowery texts full of buttercups and baby lambs. A look at the high standards to which librarians at that time held their positions disproved this theory instantly, but the fear of women holding this position of power was nevertheless present.

On the librarians' part, their purchasing choices were based on a set of standards by which all books were held accountable. This meant that some of the books that proved most popular with children were kept out of library rooms. So it was that "many a prominent librarian felt that a librarian's primary duty lay in making discriminating choices which would eliminate such trivia as the widely circulated 'dime novels' and leave only the best for young eyes and minds to absorb" (Rollock 1988, 5). Librarians weren't making "feminine" choices, but the titles they chose to exclude did happen to be read primarily by boys and young men.

During the late nineteenth century, there was also a significant increase in printed bibliographies of recommended books written by librarians so that, "during the 1880s and 1890s, children's librarians began to establish standards for juvenile library books" (Jenkins 1996). Of course, the line between endorsing "standards" and censoring choices quickly became a problem, and it remains so today. In 1881 a former minister and cataloger by the name of James M. Hubbard decided that protecting youth in libraries was of the utmost importance. Therefore, he proposed ways to keep them safe, including, "a board of censors to screen material; the labeling of harmless books; a special children's card that would permit 'children' . . . to withdraw only harmless books; and a separate children's catalog containing only permissible requests" (Geller 1984, 33). Today some librarians might find these limitations and stipulations extreme. However, some of those proposals still crop up. Periodically communities consider placing rating stickers on children or teen books. In one such example in 2005, the trustees of the Guilderland (New York) Public Library even considered a proposal to stick warning labels on young adult books with sexually explicit content (Oatman 2005). After three hours of discussion, the proposal was defeated.

TWENTIETH CENTURY: UP WITH STANDARDS

The rise of children's librarianship can also be tied directly to the state of the children's publishing industry. When taken as a whole, "technological advances in printing, the spread of compulsory education, and the consequent rise in literacy all contributed to the creation of a significant body of writing for American children by the end of the nineteenth century" (Jenkins 1996, 813–27). As publishers responded to the growing need of literature for young people, library concerns shifted. By the mid-twentieth century, librarians were concerned with keeping classics on their shelves alongside newer titles. According to Helen Nesbitt, "The core of every children's book collection, the foundation of the building, the nucleus about which the rest of the collection is built, is the group of those books which might be called standard books. These are titles which, with passage of time, will becomes classics" (1956, 27).

The number of titles written for children was increasing. As the number of books published for kids went up, it's important to examine exactly how the American children's librarians dealt with their collections. How did they sort the new from the old? What kept them up-to-date with the latest titles? What kind of review sources did they use?

Many of the review sources we use today began publication during this period. *Booklist,* a magazine that today reviews 2,500 titles a year for children, was established in 1905. Similarly, *Horn Book Magazine* came into being in 1924 and still provides some of the best information about children's literature. Librarians have subscribed to journals like these since their inception, having always been keen on getting professional opinions regarding the titles they place in the hands of children. Selection was now easier than ever before. As Anne Carroll Moore, creator of New York Public Library's Children's Services Division, said, "The principle of selection should be to provide the best standard novels . . . without lowering the standard of that taste for good reading which is the chief purpose in shelving such a collection in a children's room" (1908, 270).

When people talk about "old school" children's librarianship, they sometimes point out missteps on the part of librarians. For example, there was the case regarding *The Wonderful Wizard of Oz,* its sequels, and their exclusion from public libraries. There was a time when it was difficult to find a single copy of these books on library shelves, and for a number of reasons. In the years following the books' original publication, children's literary advocates of the 1920s and 1930s viewed fantasy warily. The books were seen as "popular" in a time when popularity was frequently considered to be in direct opposition to quality. The result of all of this was that "*Oz* was excluded from a Kansas City library in the 1920s, from the children's rooms of the New York Public Library in the 1920s (by Anne Carroll Moore), and from the open stacks of the Detroit Library in the 1950s (by Ralph Ulveling); in 1959 the state librarian of Florida encouraged public libraries to withdraw *Oz* from circulation" (Clark 2003, 133). We cannot judge these librarians too harshly. Spotting the classic stories in your midst before they are considered to be in the canon isn't as easy as people would have you believe.

Librarian and teacher W. C. Berwick Sayers said in 1932 that a good book for children "must recognize the rights of men and of animals; it should show cruelty in its own hideous features" (48). It is a noble view, but a very narrow definition when examined closely. There is no room for books like Robert Cormier's *The Chocolate War* in such a view, for example. As one of the 100 most frequently challenged books between 1990 and 2000 according to the America Library Association, *The Chocolate War* ends with the bad guys winning after a great deal of cruelty. Today we as librarians must take pains to avoid a black-and-white stance against the subtlety in our children's literature.

If your library system has created recommended reading lists over the decades, look at the past lists. They can tell you a lot about what was important to librarians then and where their priorities lay. The same can be said for large collections of children's materials in public branches. Just as it is important to remember where we have been, so too do we need to reexamine what we want to take from the past.

The librarians of the past considered issues that remain important today. What are the best review sources to consider when selecting materials? How do you balance out your collection with classics versus popular materials of outstanding quality? Is there any place in the library for guilty pleasures? Perhaps past librarians' answers to these questions were less flexible than ours today, but none of this is to say that they were wrong in their decisions.

TWENTY-FIRST CENTURY: HOW FAR WE'VE COME

The idea that the public library should merely educate and enlighten young people will never dissipate, but we have broader concerns on our plate than giving children the books we deem "the best." Walk into the children's room of a public library today, and the difference between libraries past and present is immediately apparent. Where rooms used to contain only desks, straight-backed chairs, and low tables, now we have computer terminals, comfy seating, and books for kids of all ages. A youth librarian's job back then would have consisted of a little storytelling and a lot of shelving and readers' advisory service. Now children's librarians are expected to be able to juggle a host of talents. We run computer programs and introduce traveling performers. We visit schools as often as possible to promote summer reading clubs and sign children up for library cards. We do storytimes *and* storytelling (not the same thing; I come back to that in chapter 4), and if a class of children comes in, we need to be able to give an orientation, tour, and booktalk. On top of all that, we have to be able to keep up with the latest books as well as have a sense of enduring older titles. Is it any wonder that we burn out or fall behind on keeping our readers' advisory knowledge current?

More than this, we also sometimes have to deal with people who believe that the Internet negates the necessity of libraries as a neighborhood presence. Many times the people who say this kind of thing are, unsurprisingly, not regular library users. It is possible that as our patrons grow older, they are less inclined to crack open a book, but that just means that we children's librarians have to get to the kids while they're young. In many places, the children's librarians are the bread and butter of the library system. We serve large numbers of users, and our circulation numbers are through the roof. Walk into any bookstore, and nine times out of ten you'll find the children's section in the back. Just as grocery stores put basic staples like milk and bread in the farthest corners of their buildings so that the customers have to pass other tempting, if less essential, products on their way, so too do bookstores recognize that children's books are important destinations. Rather than putting them in the front of the store, they put them in the back in the hope that adult buyers will browse on their way there. Bookstores consider children's rooms to be well-used, necessary, and profitable places.

The future is filled with both hope and fear. Librarians today now deal with a host of worries about our profession that our predecessors never had to face. Like us, they had to handle budget cuts, but what about the rise of e-books? I think we'll be okay. Although funding cuts frequently threaten librarian job security, the profession as a whole is in no danger of disappearing. As for e-books, I understand the fear that they could supplant their paper equivalents. Yet as author Sara Nelson put it so eloquently, "The e-worriers are, I predict, way wrong, just as those who worried that audio books would supplant 'real' books, and DVDs would demolish cinemas were wrong" (2008, 17). For all their charms, consider the superior technology of the picture book. You can carry it everywhere. You never have to charge it up. There is far less strain to the eyes. Cuddling up with a book at night is far simpler than cuddling up to a laptop or BlackBerry. Until that changes, librarians will be dealing with paper rather than pixels. And should necessity call for it, someday librarians may help people choose among the various e-books available for checkout through the library. They will always be around to help. The librarian of the future will simply need a certain level of flexibility and the ability to adjust to changing technology.

Editorial writers, bloggers, and electronic mailing list participants still occasionally lodge complaints about the number of women working within the librarian field. This is usually coupled with criticisms of the "feminine" literature they promote. People still want to restrict and ban children's titles that they feel have no place in a library. Selection policies found in public libraries are still used to determine the best in children's literature, though we may consider elements like sexism and racism more than our predecessors would have. Not as much has changed as we might think.

FIVE LAWS WE CAN LIVE WITH

In 1931 mathematician and librarian S. R. Ranganathan created his list of the Five Laws of Library Science. These laws represent the bedrock of library science. Child patrons are no less important than adults, and they require a different sort of attention. With that in mind, I urge you to consider the five laws of children's librarianship as adapted by Virginia A. Walter (2001, 123):

1. Libraries serve the reading interests and information needs of all children, directly and through service to parents and other adults who are involved in the lives of children.

2. Children's librarians provide the right book or information for the right child at the right time in the right place.

3. Children's librarians are advocates for children's access to books, information, information technology, and ideas.

4. Children's librarians promote children's literacy in all media.

5. Children's librarians honor their traditions and create the future.

100 Children's Books That Belong in Every Library
(Snarky Annotations Included)

No two children's librarians will ever come up with the same list of the 100 children's books for children up to age twelve that every library should own. This is my own personal list of titles and preferences that I think people (librarians as well as patrons) should seriously consider owning. They have been selected through my work with children and their presence in the literary canon. These are titles that will stand the test of time. Most, if not all, should still be in print.

Board Books (Birth to Age 2)

Board books are a tricky group to judge. In general you want books with bright colors that contrast nicely, rounded corners, and a jolly text. There are hundreds of fine and fabulous board books to choose from, but these three are my favorites.

Ten, Nine, Eight by Molly Bang—A great number book where a parent and child count various items in a room. A sweet title containing father-daughter love.

Goodnight Moon by Margaret Wise Brown—Comfort reading in the form of saying good night to various objects. I'm not personally a fan, but as bedtime fare goes, this title is famous for all the right reasons.

The Very Hungry Caterpillar by Eric Carle—A color book, number book, interactive book, and title with scientific underpinnings to boot. And it's gorgeous.

Picture Books (Ages 2 to 8)

With the understanding that these books are to be read to children when they are young and by children when they are older, here is a tiny picture book canon. I've tried to include some titles that are a bit more recent that your average *Millions of Cats* fare.

Miss Nelson Is Missing! by Harry Allard, illustrated by James Marshall—The Allard/Marshall mix gave the world its most infamous substitute teacher. I had to limit this list to 100 books, so I allowed myself only one Marshall title. *George and Martha,* I proffer to you my apologies.

Madeline by Ludwig Bemelmans—Creates a female character with just the right mix of spunk without ever becoming obnoxious. A visual stunner that also manages to read aloud brilliantly. No small feat.

The Story of Babar by Jean de Brunhoff—A little elephant goes from innocent jungle denizen to dapper man-about-town. In spite of accusations of colonial underpinnings (to say nothing of the abundant dead elephants), Babar's snazzy style and charm are fit for any library collection.

The Rabbit and the Turtle by Eric Carle—If you had to pick only one collection of Aesop's fables to include in your collection, go with the one created by the only children's book illustrator to have his own museum.

Abuela by Arthur Dorros, illustrated by Elisa Kleven—A girl's relationship with her grandmother takes to the sky. Offering Spanish and English terms alongside one another, this beautiful tale is both touching and a wonderful read.

Wilfred Gordon McDonald Partridge by Mem Fox, illustrated by Julie Vivas—A boy befriends an elderly woman whose memory is fading. "Issue" books are difficult to write and even harder to read. Fox's is one of the best of the lot, and illustrator Julie Vivas (to my mind) should be canonized at some point.

Millions of Cats by Wanda Gág—A man comes home with more than his fair share of felines in tow. An oldie, a goodie, and one of those books that will get stuck in your head forever.

Lilly's Purple Plastic Purse by Kevin Henkes—Lilly's relationship with her beloved teacher is strained when her antics lead to punishment. Lilly is one of the rare self-absorbed preschool heroines who can act naughty and indulgent without sacrificing personality for sympathy.

The Snowy Day by Ezra Jack Keats—The premise sounds simple: a boy plays in the snow. But it was considered a groundbreaking book when Keats made his small hero a black child. Now the book's look at the beauty of urban living and city environments serves as a rare sight on bookstore and library shelves today.

The Story of Ferdinand by Munro Leaf, illustrated by Robert Lawson—A young bull prefers smelling flowers to goring matadors. It has been accused of anti-American pacifism, so you know it *has* to be good.

Swimmy by Leo Lionni—A small black fish finds acceptance through difference. Though Lionni is better remembered for his mice, *Swimmy* remains his masterpiece due to its take on brains over brawn and a look at making differences work within the context of society.

Brown Bear, Brown Bear, What Do You See? by Bill Martin Jr., illustrated by Eric Carle—Storytime staple teaching colors and animals, and with it Carle makes his third appearance on my list. But seriously? How could I have the heart not to include it?

Chicka Chicka Boom Boom by Bill Martin Jr., illustrated by John Archambault—The alphabet rendered in a catchy, bouncy, goofy format. This one got hit hard with the "future classic" stick. If you haven't discovered it already, then you are out of the loop.

Make Way for Ducklings by Robert McCloskey—Two ducks attempt to find a safe place to raise their brood and, let's admit it, fail. Charges of sexism briefly dogged this fabulous tale (Mr. Duck gets to go on a walkabout while Mrs. Duck stays home with the little duckies), but in the end it's the quintessential story of ducks and traffic congestion.

And Tango Makes Three by Peter Parnell and Justin Richardson, illustrated by Henry Cole—Based on a true story, two male penguins raise a chick of their own. I've few informational books on this list and fewer titles with gay-friendly themes. Technically, *Tango* meets both of these needs and happens to be a great book as well.

The Tale of Peter Rabbit by Beatrix Potter—A naughty little rabbit gets his comeuppance. Potter made the book tiny for tiny hands. There is no denying the charm of the crisp language and scientifically accurate (albeit clothed) bunny rabbits in this story.

Curious George by H. A. Rey—Another naughty animal, this time in the form of a monkey. Personally I can take this cheeky simian or leave him, but I sense potential outrage at his exclusion. And so on this list he crouches, grinning maniacally.

Where the Wild Things Are by Maurice Sendak—A boy's fantasy at acting out leads to his kingship in foreign lands. Every psychoanalytic report and academic thesis to pry this book apart inevitably ends up at the same conclusion: Book good. Read book.

Caps for Sale by Esphyr Slobodkina—A salesman runs into trouble when monkeys foist his wares. The shame of my life is that I encountered Slobodkina's tale only in my adulthood. Weirdo monkey noises aside, this is a king of the read-alouds.

Chato and the Party Animals by Gary Soto, illustrated by Susan Guevara—Barrio boys in feline form is such a bizarre concept that it manages to work like a dream in this tale of miscommunication. A plethora of Spanish-language terms and phrases doesn't hurt matters.

Mufaro's Beautiful Daughters by John Steptoe—Two girls vie for the hand of a handsome prince. No list of this sort is complete without a little Steptoe in the mix. The fable's strong to begin with; in his hands, it takes on a magical quality.

Jumanji by Chris Van Allsburg—Speaking of magical qualities, I suppose we could go back and forth all day on which Van Allsburg offering is the strongest. My vote goes to the one with the tsetse fly.

Alexander and the Terrible, Horrible, No Good, Very Bad Day by Judith Viorst, illustrated by Ray Cruz—Child-friendly child psychology with a kid having the worst possible day on record. Schadenfreude allows young readers the dual privilege of sympathizing with Alexander's pain and secretly chortling over the fact that it isn't happening to them.

Don't Let the Pigeon Drive the Bus by Mo Willems—A bird attempts to talk readers into letting him into a driver's seat. Taking seeming simplicity to another level, Willems smashes down the fourth wall and creates an icon for the new millennium. A wheeling-dealing icon at that.

A Chair for My Mother by Vera B. Williams—A girl and her mother scrimp and save to get the perfect chair. Normally children's authors are reluctant to portray working-class characters unless they exist in a historical setting. Williams tromps that trend and tugs at the heartstrings without cloying or pandering.

Show Way by Jacqueline Woodson, illustrated by Hudson Talbott—Woodson follows her own family history through several generations. It could have won for its pictures, but Woodson's personal story was a Newbery Honor book for a reason: the woman can write.

Lon Po Po by Ed Young—Young's masterpiece. This Little Red Riding Hood tale somehow manages to be even creepier than the original while simultaneously being less disturbing.

Books for Beginning Readers (Ages 5 to 7)

When a child looks at you with all the pent-up frustration of an early reader, it is wise to acquiesce to his or her reading levels. These books will give them the substance they need while still remaining cool.

Are You My Mother? by P. D. Eastman—A newborn searches tirelessly for his mom. Actually, my brother-in-law despises this title. But whereas he finds the barren, motherless landscape treacherous and forbidding, I love how Eastman's plucky bird hero searches for his heart's desire without a smidgen of self-pity or despair.

Frog and Toad Are Friends by Arthur Lobel—Two friends have small adventures. Words do not do it justice. If there is such a thing as a perfect beginning reader book, this is it.

The Cat in the Hat by Dr. Seuss—A dangerous playmate proves to two children that you should be careful what you wish for. Anarchic top-hatted felines aside, Seuss's book uses some basic words in a format that finally put the kibosh on good old Dick and Jane.

My Friend Is Sad by Mo Willems—Piggie attempts to cheer up her friend without realizing that she's making matters worse. A comedy duo for the lollipop set. Parents have been known to stifle chuckles when reading these on subways as well.

Books for Young Readers (Ages 7 to 9)

And then suddenly they're too cool for books without chapter headings. Before you go tossing them 700-page fantasy tomes, however, consider handing them a couple of these fine and fancy early chapter books. All the words they want with a couple of pictures as well for comfort.

Hans Christian Andersen's Fairy Tales, selected and illustrated by Lisbeth Zwerger, translated by Anthea Bell—Choosing a favorite Andersen collection often comes down to finding the right translator. I trust Bell intrinsically, and Zwerger's uncanny sense of what makes up the heart of these tales renders her art the perfect match.

Tales of a Fourth Grade Nothing by Judy Blume—A fourth grader must deal with his little brother's antics. There isn't an older sibling alive who won't feel comforted and justified by Blume's dead-on sympathy for those who have the misfortune to be born first.

The Stories Julian Tells by Ann Cameron—A boy and his exaggerations provide the background to these short stories. If you take the beating and whipping jokes in the book with a grain of salt, Julian provides the right sure-footedness and cocky attitude you need in a master of exaggeration.

My Father's Dragon by Ruth Stiles Gannett, illustrated by Ruth Chrisman Gannett—The narrator's father goes to an island to rescue a baby dragon from its captors. It's remarkable how this one keeps chugging along through the years, and I've certainly never found a faster way to render third graders mute.

Toys Go Out by Emily Jenkins, illustrated by Paul Zelinsky—Three toys live through several adventures. There are many tales of sentient toys but few with this level of pathos and wry humor.

The Tales of Uncle Remus: The Adventures of Brer Rabbit as told by Julius Lester, illustrated by Jerry Pinkney—If you can't trust Lester to get to the bottom of the Brer Rabbit tales, then whom can you trust? Uncle Remus has been revived in an entirely new manner.

The Year of the Dog by Grace Lin—A Taiwanese American girl navigates friendships and problems in school. Not since Laura Ingalls Wilder has an author so perfectly captured the magic in the protagonist's everyday life. Lin is a wonder.

Ruby Lu, Brave and True by Lenore Look, illustrated by Anne Wilsdorf—Short stories about Chinese school and reflective tape. Spunky heroines are difficult to write without falling into facetious or twee territory. This gal will never be considered a knockoff Ramona, however, and her energy is superb.

Sarah, Plain and Tall by Patricia MacLachlan—Homestead children meet their father's bride. Also sometimes known as "the short Newbery winner." And what it lacks in length it makes up for in incisive, smart, remarkable writing. Brevity in motion.

Captain Underpants by Dav Pilkey—Two boys hypnotize their principal into becoming a superhero. How can I help but include him? Even if he wasn't catnip to reluctant readers, there's always room on the shelf for potty humor when it's done with such panache.

Pink and Say by Patricia Polacco—The story of two friends during the Civil War. You could also put it in the picture book section of your library, but really it deserves a space of its own. When people ask me for a good, easy book for teens or adults who are learning to read, this is the book I go to.

Seasons by Charlotte Zolotow, illustrated by Erik Blegvad—Poems about the seasons. Entirely a personal choice on my part, but this book evokes such remarkable sensations that I simply had to include it.

Books for Middle Readers (Ages 8 to 11)

Although school assignments will mean that most of these are read anyway, be sure to find a way to press some of these goodies into the hands of kids who might say, "What's a tollbooth?" when you mention Juster's greatest.

The Book of Three by Lloyd Alexander—A quintessential fairy tale complete with headstrong hero, outspoken maiden, scatterbrained bard, and odd, furry thing that really likes to eat.

Tuck Everlasting by Natalie Babbitt—A family and their dealings with eternal life. Probably contains the most misleadingly slow beginning of any children's novel I know, but Babbitt's book is a classic for a reason. Eerie and wonderful.

The Wonderful Wizard of Oz by Frank L. Baum, illustrated by Michael Hague—Why include it? Because because because because because . . . because of the wonderful things it does. And to see how different it is from the movie too, for that matter.

Caddie Woodlawn by Carol Ryrie Brink, illustrated by Trina Schart Hyman—A fiery redhead and her pioneer life. Of course, it has to handle its fair share of cries of racism in terms of the American Indian characters, but I've always felt that *Caddie* gets a bad rap.

Wabi by Joseph Bruchac—An owl falls in love with a beautiful human girl. And to my mind, you can never have enough superhero American Indians. All of Bruchac's humor and romance with a slam-bang story as well.

The Secret Garden by Frances Hodgson Burnett, illustrated by Inga Moore—Quite possibly the world's most perfect children's book. Gothic, heartwarming, and with two protagonists you'd love to kick in the shins until they find their ecological redemption. Choose whichever version you prefer, though I'm a fan of illustrator Inga Moore's take.

Ramona the Pest by Beverly Cleary, illustrated by Louis Darling—The world according to a girl just beginning school. Often emulated and copied every single year, but never to be replaced. Ramona now and forever, amen.

The Dark Is Rising by Susan Cooper—A boy discovers his fantastical legacy. Technically it was the second book in the Dark Is Rising series, but this is the title where the magic really is afoot. Worth a reread if you haven't had a chance to peruse it in a while.

The Watsons Go to Birmingham—1963 by Christopher Paul Curtis—Small stories about an African American family, culminating in a tense visit to Birmingham at an explosive time. If you would like to see historical fiction done well, look no further.

Charlie and the Chocolate Factory by Roald Dahl, illustrated by Quentin Blake—A boy, a chocolate factory, and a potentially insane proprietor. Several people have equated sex in adult literature to food in children's. Candy, however, is a realm in and of itself, and only Dahl could have mixed in unpreachy moralizing this dark and delightful.

Half Magic by Edward Eager, illustrated by N. M. Bodecker—What if you found an object that would grant you half your wishes? Behold girls as knights and cats that can half talk. If this doesn't charm you, nothing will.

The Birchbark House by Louise Erdrich—Erdrich gave the Little House franchise a run for its money when she began this amazing and delightful series about American Indians in the Upper Midwest. Funny and heartbreaking by turns.

Harriet the Spy by Louise Fitzhugh—Spying on your friends and family can lead to complications, it seems. Features an unlikable heroine who manages to inspire a whole generation of girls to keep journals of their own. If that isn't a testament to good writing, what is?

The Whipping Boy by Sid Fleischman, illustrated by Peter Sís—A whipping boy and his prince find themselves up to their ears in adventure. Competes with *Sarah, Plain and Tall* for the title of "Most Preferred Short Newbery Winner." *Raucous, fun,* and *exciting* are other words you might use to describe it.

Joey Pigza Swallowed the Key by Jack Gantos—Children everywhere with attention deficit disorder or attention deficit hyperactivity disorder found their spokesman in Joey, a kid who manages to charm you even while he's bouncing off the walls and driving you insane.

The Wind in the Willows by Kenneth Grahame, illustrated by Inga Moore—One of the first novels for children to put clothes on animals. Various edited versions prove quite popular, as do those with well-illustrated full texts.

The People Could Fly: American Black Folktales by Virginia Hamilton, illustrated by Leo and Diane Dillon—Tales of African Americans are coupled with Dillon and Dillon's smooth, insightful pictures. Hamilton's voice rings cool and clear on every page, enticing readers to find her other works.

Redwall by Brian Jacques—Abbey mice fight a team of nasty rats in this breathtaking beginning to a series. As I always say, if you want to write a series about adults for children, just make those adults furry woodland creatures. Jacques is a master storyteller, and his hit series begins with a magnificent bang.

The Phantom Tollbooth by Norton Juster, illustrated by Jules Feiffer—A bored boy finds himself in an alternate world. The Juster/Feiffer pairing brings this ribald satire into full-breathing life.

Isaac Newton by Kathleen Krull, illustrated by Boris Kulikov—A better biography of Newton for kids I have not seen. A brilliant, fun, and funny read. Everything nonfiction should attempt to be.

A Wizard of Earthsea by Ursula K. Le Guin—A self-centered boy finds that magic isn't as easy to control as he thought it was. Le Guin did wizarding schools before it was cool. Better still, she was good at them.

A Wrinkle in Time by Madeleine L'Engle—A girl and two boys attempt to rescue her father from evil otherworldly forces. Writers, do not try this at home! The mixing of science fiction *and* religion is tricky at best, car wrecky at worst. L'Engle's success in this arena can be attributed to her mad skills.

The Lion, the Witch, and the Wardrobe by C. S. Lewis— Speaking of mixing religion into your works, Lewis wasn't afraid of making his metaphor shockingly obvious to adults and entirely invisible to children. The idea of kids entering an alternate fantasy world is hard to top in this one.

Pippi Longstocking by Astrid Lindgren, illustrated by Lauren Child—A wild girl with her own horse entertains the local tots. To my mind, Pippi is the original child superhero. Super strength, tons of money, her own monkey. What more could any child want?

Rules by Cynthia Lord—A girl deals with her little brother's autism and gaining the acceptance of the new girl on the block. Lord's pitch-perfect storytelling takes the difficult subject of autism and works it into a universal tale of friends and siblings.

Number the Stars by Lois Lowry—A child helps save some Jewish people in World War II Denmark. It's always very difficult to make the Holocaust a subject that is comprehensible to children. Lowry's is perhaps one of the smartest, and her storytelling abilities shine on every page.

The New Way Things Work by David Macaulay—Inventions, sound, even digital aspects are all explained in Macaulay's signature style. Informational books are rarely so intriguing. Macaulay has a way with concrete objects and mechanics that few match and fewer still try.

Winnie-the-Pooh by A. A. Milne, illustrated by E. Shepard— A boy and his bear in a book that manages to be cute without being twee. A way to attempt to banish Disney's version from the minds of young readers.

Mrs. Frisby and the Rats of NIMH by Robert C. O'Brien—
A mouse turns to artificially intelligent rats to help
her in her hour of need. Science fiction is rarely this
engaging. A book that takes the whole talking mice
idea and turns it entirely on its head. Wonderfully
dark.

Bridge to Terabithia by Katherine Paterson—A boy and a girl
become friends, creating their own imaginary world.
While some kids encounter their first literary death in
Charlotte's Web, others hit it in this stark and haunting
tale. One of the finest novels there is.

The Higher Power of Lucky by Susan Patron, illustrated by
Matt Phelan—A girl attempts to find "home" with
her guardian in the smallest town imaginable. Full of
subtle human moments, this delicious story of Lucky's
struggle and life becomes much more than the sum of
its parts.

Hatchet by Gary Paulsen—To my mind, Paulsen is the Ernest
Hemingway of children's books. And no title backs this
theory up better than his harrowing tale of one boy's
fight for survival in the wilderness.

Harry Potter and the Sorcerer's Stone by J. K. Rowling—
A boy discovers that he is a wizard. Love the series
or hate it (and I love it), Harry is unavoidable and
undeniably popular. The fact that the books are
incredibly fun doesn't hurt matters any either.

Holes by Louis Sachar—This isn't just the story of a boy
named Stanley Yelnats. This is the story of America
(she said without irony). To my mind, the best
Newbery Medal winner in the past twenty years.

Where the Sidewalk Ends by Shel Silverstein—Twisted
poetry from the craziest children's author out there. I
had a hard time deciding between this and *A Light in*

the Attic, but I think the poem about Sarah Cynthia Sylvia Stout alone breaks the tie.

The Arrival by Shaun Tan—An immigrant attempts to make a new life in a strange world. Convinced that a wordless graphic novel (or is it a wordless novel?) can't make you cry? Think again.

Roll of Thunder, Hear My Cry by Mildred Taylor—Fourth grader Cassie Logan deals with racism in the 1930s American South. One of the true children's literary epics and a blunt introduction to racism.

Team Moon: How 400,000 People Landed Apollo 11 on the Moon by Catherine Thimmesh—A gripping nonfiction play-by-play of the people responsible for the moon landing. A breathtaking book.

Charlotte's Web by E. B. White, illustrated by Garth Williams—A pig and a spider strike up an unlikely friendship. For many, it's the book that gently introduced them to the concept of death. For others, it's an almost perfect barnyard tale.

Little House in the Big Woods by Laura Ingalls Wilder, illustrated by Garth Williams—Mothers, don't let your babies grow up to not read at least one Little House book. And if you read any of them, you may as well begin at the beginning.

Books for Older Readers (Ages 11 to 12)

Chains by Laurie Halse Anderson—A slave in colonial America finds that neither the British nor the Americans have her best interests at heart. Pulse pounding and an excellent corrective to anyone who sees this moment in history in terms of good guys versus bad guys.

The Hunger Games by Suzanne Collins—Children compete to stay alive in a dark and distant future. Gripping. Violent. Intense. Unforgettable from cover to cover.

Phineas Gage: A Gruesome but True Story of Brain Science by John Fleischman—The true tale of one man's close association with a six-foot pole and the hole it left in his brain. Quite possibly my favorite book to booktalk.

Lincoln: A Photobiography by Russell Freedman—When they ask you for a Lincoln biography, this is the one to hand over time and time again. The rare nonfiction Newbery Medal winner.

The House of Dies Drear by Virginia Hamilton—A great ghost story and mystery with the Underground Railroad worked in for spice.

The Outsiders by S. E. Hinton—Rich and poor boys fight for their lives. Even if you remember that Hinton wrote this when she was sixteen, you will hardly be able to believe it. One of the few books for young readers that actively deal with class.

The Giver by Lois Lowry—A boy takes on the memories of his community. Allegory done right (and that's no small task). Once you've finished reading it, you can decide what to make of the ending on your own.

Anne of Green Gables by L. M. Montgomery—A girl searches for "home" while wrangling with her own overactive imagination. The world's most popular Canadian redhead in her first (and best, if you ask me) tale.

Bad Boy: A Memoir by Walter Dean Myers—Myers records his own boyhood in 1940s Harlem. I bet a lot of people would fill this list to brimming with Walter Dean Myers if you asked them to. And if you need a good autobiography, then this is probably the one to pick.

The Westing Game by Ellen Raskin—A game that could lead to riches in the end. It's hard to find people who aren't a fan of this one, as evidenced by the many, many reissues and editions it's associated with. If we were to play the What's the Most Popular Newbery Medal Winner game, this might even give *Holes* a run for its money.

Good Masters! Sweet Ladies! Voices from a Medieval Village by Laura Amy Schlitz—Twenty-two monologues written in the voices of children living in an English village. Not only will this come in handy for your students who need audition and forensic pieces, but it is also a fun, factual, downright amusing ride as well. And that shiny medal on the cover doesn't hurt matters much either.

The Hobbit by J. R. R. Tolkien—A small creature called a hobbit goes on adventures against his will. I suppose that I could have added one of the other Lord of the Rings books if I'd wanted to, but sometimes it's a good idea to begin at the beginning.

Homecoming by Cynthia Voigt—Child abandonment and an epic quest to find "home." Raises the great children's fear of what would happen if your mom left you in a car in a parking lot and then never came back.

American Born Chinese by Gene Luen Yang—A boy tries to fit in with the other kids in his school. It was hard to pick and choose among the many graphic novels, but if Yang's story is anything, it's a deft look at assimilation and the price of giving up your soul to be like everyone else.

TWO

Standards and Quality in Literature

Bernice Cullinan and Lee Galda's must-read book *Literature and the Child* contains a section in the first chapter titled "The Value of Literature." In it, the authors systematically recount what it is that great literature gives children. Through books, children increase their language growth and development, become better readers and writers, learn to love reading, explore their feelings, and learn about diversity. And so they conclude, "The richness and diversity that typifies literature today means that teachers, librarians, parents, and young people have a wealth of books from which to select" (2002, 8). However you define "the best," you know that it's precisely what you want to give your young patrons. Yet how do you decide whether to purchase for your collection that which is good versus that which is popular? The solution is in the balance.

Does quality matter? In this day and age of circulation statistics, are librarians still the arbiters of what books constitute worthwhile reading? There are two schools of thought on the matter. Some believe that the time of the judgmental librarian is past. Since libraries are increasingly reliant on circulation statistics to maintain their funding, it is difficult to justify choosing only "the best" for our small patrons. Other schools of thought say that if librarians don't separate the good from the bad as they see it, who will? I believe that these two takes are not incompatible. It is possible to include titles of lesser quality alongside those of high quality without sacrificing your expertise or the library's high standards of literature. What you need to determine, however, is what constitutes "quality."

In the past, quality was seen as more than just a way of distinguishing a good book from a bad book. It was defined as how best a human life could be lived. High-quality literature was seen to be the kind of thing that could reform and promote better learning and living.

As a librarian, you are going to face a certain expectation that you can distinguish good books from bad books. And you are going to have field requests for quality books. So how do you go about finding them? For that matter, what are they? The term *quality literature* is bandied about by librarians in the field yet is pretty vague when you get right down to it. What makes one book for kids any better than another? How do you go about determining what is good? And why should it even matter? Often it seems as though the collective sigh among parents these days is, "As long as they're reading," and I understand this mode of thought. When you are presented with a child more entranced by glowing screens than thick, creamy pages, you may fall into apoplexies of unrestrained joy when that same child starts paging through a new edition of *Mad Libs*.

Parents and teachers are always asking children's librarians for recommendations because it is important to introduce children to great

How did the library select books in the past?

[In the past] we used to use only staff reviews for everything on three-by-five multiple form slips, and we still have a file of reviews. Then demand increased for series books, more "popular" items, and there was a huge demand for Clifford picture books, which we did not buy. Now, of course, we've gone quite the other way. We buy many series, particularly in paperback, and we buy less and less ordinary, undistinguished, run-of-the-mill hardcover fiction because it sits on the shelf. I'm more careful, especially with quantities, and especially with historical fiction. And especially with books that have sepia-toned covers because they sit on the shelf. We always reviewed everything. If it's a continuing book in a series, we're not as likely to review it.

Susan Pine, materials specialist, New York Public Library

What is "quality" children's literature?

Since I read and evaluate lots of children's literature myself, I feel very comfortable going with my gut instinct about what is quality and what is not, but at the same time I'm always interested in what other people think is quality, so I consult review journals, award lists, and other professional opinions offered on blogs and electronic mailing lists. I do prefer to purchase these items, but not exclusively. With increasingly limited budgets, I really need to buy things that are also popular with students, so I'm looking—and aren't we all?—for those books that have quality and popularity.

Jonathan Hunt, elementary school librarian,
Modesto City Schools district, California

works of children's literature. Former editor of *Horn Book Magazine* Anita Silvey says, "Just as every literate adult knows certain books, every child should know specific children's books. If we fail to present these books to children, they reach adulthood without a basic literary heritage" (2004, x). A child growing up in America entirely ignorant of *Where the Wild Things Are* or having only a passing familiarity with Roald Dahl misses out on essential cultural touchstones. When I go to a party full of people outside the children's literary sphere, I sometimes like to start conversations with, "So what was your favorite kids' book when you were growing up?" because many of us have this single point in common.

I believe firmly in the existence and use of great children's literature, but personally I think that there's a lot to be said for schlock too. My own childhood was as full of classics like *The Wind in the Willows* and *The Lion, the Witch, and the Wardrobe* but also cheap comic books and tie-ins to cartoons and movies. My parents gave me a healthy mix so that I'd spend some of my summer vacation reading *Voyage of the Dawn Treader* and then put it down to devour a Choose Your Own Adventure novel or an *Ewoks* comic book. It was from Archie comics that I learned what a palindrome is and from Asterix and Obelix the existence of the Gauls. As my mother always said, there is often something new to learn in a comic.

Let's examine comic books and graphic novels. When we discuss what is and isn't quality, comics are particularly divisive among librarians, and that has a lot to do with the fact that the quality varies considerably. A lot of librarians feel that comics have no place in a library due to shoddy storytelling, poor drawing, and weak binding. It is important to remember, though, that there are different kinds of comics and graphic novels. I mentioned that I grew up reading *Ewoks* comics and similar fare—these were materials that were intended to be ephemeral. You read 'em, you toss 'em. End of story. Yet soon people started to ascribe a great deal of value to those comics that used to have seemingly little or no value. The artistic merits of a Superman or Batman comic book entered the conversation. But there are other kinds of comics as well. Artists began working in the comic and graphic novel field with purposefully high-quality products produced with a great deal of care and effort in terms of their story and the illustrations. That leaves a children's librarian with a lot of questions to answer. Do I want to purchase only new graphic novels and eschew the comics of the past because they were not meant to be seen as works of quality literature? Do I buy large numbers of classic collections because there are people today who view them as works of art? Or do I consider everything comics related to be junk?

When I'm out in the field touting the best graphic novels for kids for all that they are worth, the number one question I get from my skeptical audience members is whether these books will make their children better readers of prose. If you have a child who will read the *Bone* graphic novels by Jeff Smith one after another without ceasing, does it mean that they are going to tackle Tolkien's Lord of the Rings series? I like to think so. I have known kids who could move from the visual and literary to the merely literary without much difficulty. Still, I'd like to make it clear that many graphic novels are worthy additions to a collection in their own right rather than extras to be reluctantly tacked on to the fiction section.

How do you select books in your library?

All of the children's librarians [in the San Francisco Public Library system] review books, and there's a revolving monthly book evaluation committee to help determine what goes on our monthly ordering list. I have to say that as wonderful as this is, it's gotten a bit difficult to keep up with the purity of intent. We're all just too busy, and children's publishing has exploded so. Books with buzz, series books, respected authors and illustrators, and patron requests all get added to our lists these days.

Carla Kozak, San Francisco Public Library

I am absolutely of the opinion that there can be gold in books or materials that some people would label as junk. Libraries in particular have a different set of standards in place. And although I feel that librarians should embrace the comic revolution, you shouldn't go out of your way to provide materials you consider to be tripe. The poet Walter de la Mare once said, "Only the rarest kind of best in anything can be good enough for the young." That means that if you are going to provide something for your juvenile community, it should be good. Quality. Worthwhile reading.

In terms of collection development, many librarians (and I am one of them) believe themselves to be standard-bearers. And in many ways we are. You will find Scooby-Doo and Disney storybooks in some collections, but many librarians aren't happy with including them. The temptation is to provide the same books kids would choose to buy in a bookstore. Personally, I have always felt that libraries should be more than merely free versions of large corporate-owned bookstores. That said, it is important to remember that over time, standards change. In her book *From Cover to Cover,* author K. T. Horning argues that the question, "What makes a good children's book?" is difficult to answer because of the sheer variety. But she says, "As times change and our perception of children evolves, so too do our standards for excellence in children's books" (1997, x). Some libraries today fear comics in spite of their literary significance. The question then becomes, By what standards do we define great works of literature for children?

Complicating the matter is the eternal debate between quality and user statistics. Quantifying a library's usefulness in its community is difficult. Sometimes the best a system can do is to record numbers. The number of reference questions asked. The number of patrons walking through the doors. The number that will prove most interesting to community and library boards, however, is the number of library materials checked out in a given month. With that in mind, the temptation is to provide only materials that the public will read and watch voraciously. On the children's level, this comes in direct conflict with our understanding of what constitutes great literature. The solution is to find a balance.

How do you go about creating a children's collection that provides quality literature but also listens to the needs and wants of its young patrons? Generally I advise that a children's room find a natural mix of high-quality titles and mediocre series. In the Children's Center at 42nd Street in New York City, popular series books have their own separate section, as do graphic novels. When asked, the library will look into a new series, sometimes purchasing a patron's series recommendation unless the books are particularly terrible or based on a television show. As these series fall out of favor, they are weeded out and replaced by other cheap paperback series. As for graphic novels, this is an area where I feel that quality is inconsistent, and I am pleased that the library system has taken pains to ensure that only the best comics are purchased for the children's rooms of the New York Public Library by systematically examining each title and taking into consideration professional reviews. That way, we can ensure that the books that end up in the hands of our patrons are the best, as they deserve.

Great Baby Book Recommendations

Recommending books for the tiniest of tots can be downright difficult. Readers' advisory is always hard when these patrons would rather chew on than read the book in front of them. Just the same, here are a couple of staples my library has had luck with over the years.

For 0–3 months

Books Are for Reading by Suzy Becker—A sly little book that encourages kids not to chew on books, all the while sporting rubber corners for just that very purpose. If you circulate it, be sure to clean it regularly.

Barnyard Banter by Denise Fleming—For children this age, rhythm and rhyme are incredibly important. And no other board book embodies rhythm better than this jovial, catchy title.

White on Black by Tana Hoban—Clear, contrasting tones are particularly good for babies' vision, and it doesn't get much contrastier than black and white.

For 3–6 months

Scratch and Sniff: Garden from DK Publishing—Oh, it's a gimmick all right. But sensory experiences stick with babies particularly well. And scratch-and-sniff smell technology has come a long way since I was a kid.

Hand, Hand, Fingers, Thumb by Al Perkins—Catchy, rhythmic, and a great way to introduce children to their digits. It's all about reading to a beat.

Baby Faces from Playskool Books—Faces are thrilling to babies right around this age, so let's give the tots exactly what they want.

Tails by Matthew Van Fleet—Tactile, furry, fuzzy, and smooth. At long last, babies can indulge in the tail pulling they'll have to avoid when a real living kitty is in the vicinity.

For 6–9 months

Where Is Baby's Belly Button? by Karen Katz—Though they're still a little young for it, babies at this age begin to enjoy lift-the-flap books. And I would be loath not to include something by Katz, queen of the lift-the-flap world.

Helen Oxenbury's Big Baby Book by Helen Oxenbury—This is actually five of Oxenbury's board books in one. Even so, it's a mere twelve pages long, and nobody else on earth does babies as well as Oxenbury. No one.

Who Said Moo? by Harriet Ziefert, illustrated by Simms Taback—Animal sounds with just enough of a story to keep mommy and daddy from complete and utter boredom when reading and rereading.

For 9–12 months

Sounds on the Farm by Gail Donovan, illustrated by Laura Ovresat—Also a gimmick book, but a clever one. Animal sounds, *actual* animal sounds, accompany pictures of barnyard denizens.

Run, Mouse, Run! by Petr Horáček—Cutaway pages allow readers to follow a mouse as he runs through, over, under, and across. Bright colors and a fun story too.

Up, Up, Up by Emily Jenkins, illustrated by Tomek Bogacki—
Very sweet with the kind of repetition babies crave.
The Bea and HaHa series is one of the cutest out there
for babes.

ABC by Matthew Porter—This one's for the hipster parents.
It's an alphabet board book, sure, but with a design
aesthetic perfect for people looking for something a
little different.

THREE

Finding Great Children's Books

I t's not "your room" in the sense that you own any of the books there, but it's difficult not to feel a certain sense of proprietary rights when you take on a library collection. It can feel like your home away from home, a place mysterious to outsiders, where you, the children's librarian, are sometimes considered to be the sole individual with both the knowledge of the layout and the necessary insight into which of the books falling under your purview is going to be the best for each reader. The more you learn about the layout and the individual volumes, the better enabled you are to be a good and helpful librarian. You may even grow protective of your space. Whether it's a magnificent collection housing every possible topic or a single shelf of books with a limited, if precisely maintained, scope, you want to be as familiar with your materials as possible. That goes for the books you already own, as well as the books you hope to add.

GETTING WHAT YOU NEED

Unfortunately, not all library systems allow individual librarians the chance to significantly alter their own collections. It's not uncommon for larger library systems to centralize their ordering procedures, placing purchasing decisions in the hands of a very few individuals rather than branch librarians. A variety of reasons determine such decisions, but essentially the idea is that the larger a library system is, the more difficult it is for an individual librarian to balance collection development with day-to-day activities. If librarians are conducting storytimes and class visits, doing reference desk work, and filling in on desks in other parts of the library, how much time will they have for collection development as well? Still, children's librarians should know their collection, even if they have no choice about the final decision behind each purchase. Librarians work with the collections they have and strive to attain the collection they need. That means learning as much as you can about the books you're being sent and discovering additional titles that you can suggest to the person purchasing children's materials.

Every public library's children's collection, large or small, should have three distinct parts: old books, new books, and books specifically to meet a community's needs. The old and new will be titles that you, the librarian, are solely responsible for finding and distributing. The community's needs will be evident from your reference interviews and collection assessment.

Older titles can be split into several categories: award winners, classic titles (not necessarily the same thing as award winners), and

Where do you start when evaluating a collection?

Walk in the front door (not the employee entrance) and pretend you're, say, four years old. Look at the walls, floor, countertops, shelves, and displays from your eye level of approximately three feet. You cannot read any of the signage. Do you feel welcome? How far into the building do you get before you see something that lets you know that there are materials and programs especially for you? Do this exercise again, this time with the eyes of an eight-year-old who hates school. What distinguishes your institution from the one he dislikes? Continue to test the environment, imagining yourself a young mom with a beginner's knowledge of English, a shy tween, and others. Collection development is largely about access, and this walk-through should give you insight as to how accessible your library (and its resources) feels to your target clients.

Susan Patron, formerly juvenile materials collection development manager, Los Angeles Public Library, and author of The Higher Power of Lucky *(Atheneum/Richard Jackson, 2006)*

sentimental favorites. These categories may overlap from time to time, but they are hardly the same. Award winners are books that struck a particular group of adults as the best product of a given year. Whether that year in question was strong or weak is not taken into account at the time the honor is given and is evident only years later in hindsight. There are strong award winners and weak award winners, and you will have to decide which ones to keep in your collection.

Classics are different. A classic is a book that may or may not have won an award, but it has certainly stood the test of time. Of course, you may be personally opposed to some of those books cooed over by colleagues and the public alike. Just the same, they are an important part of any collection.

As for sentimental favorites, some older books are so beloved that it does not matter if they are not the best-written books of a given year. They are remembered, and they are loved. Enid Blyton is a difficult author to read if you did not grow up with her, but if you did, then you would find it shocking if she is not included in your local library's collection. Every children's room must make at least a little space for such favorites. There is no possible way to include everything beloved by everybody, but certainly a couple of titles can be included without too much fuss and bother.

THE COLLECTION: FIND OUT WHAT YOU HAVE; DISCARD WHAT YOU DON'T NEED

I have little doubt that plenty of children's librarians love every single part of their library collection. They harbor no favorites, adoring historical fiction and early reader titles just as much as they do books about drag racing and Harry Potter. However, to my mind, these librarians are the lucky few. Most librarians I know prefer one aspect of a children's room to another. They either read and adore all the new picture books coming out or they live to see the newest nonfiction titles. Some like the classics, and some prefer everything hot off the presses. For most of us, our collections are going to reflect our own personal loves and prejudices, despite our best efforts to stay open-minded. Our real job, then, is to overcome these feelings so as to have a children's collection that reflects all points of view and interests.

A children's room is not a space into which titles have been thrown higgledy-piggledy either. Said Helen Nesbitt, associate dean of the Carnegie Library School, in 1956, "A book collection, even a departmental book collection, is not merely an aggregate of miscellaneous titles. It is also . . . a construction in which each single unit is in itself a thing of balance and completeness and yet loses itself in its contribution to the whole." Balance and completeness: that is what we strive for in our children's room and, as Nesbitt points out, as part of the larger public library system. Each distinct element contributes to the larger whole. A good children's room supports a balance of topics and materials specifically purchased for the purpose of meeting the community's particular needs. A small branch in the Bronx isn't going to sport a large section of books relating to the history of Fort Worth, Texas, after all.

First, you need to determine the needs of your community. Before you can grow comfortable with purchasing new books, you need to know whether the old ones are still doing their job. And so the specter of weeding raises its ugly mug. Weeding is often simultaneously wrenching and rewarding. As a librarian, my instinct is to have every possible book on hand so that when a patron comes in looking for a biography of Jonas Salk from 1955, doggone it, we're going to have one. This is an understandable impulse, and were we librarians blessed with infinite shelves and space, it wouldn't be a problem. However, for most of us, space is an issue, as is use. Our libraries rely on high circulation statistics, and when you have vast shelves of books that are sitting there without being checked out, that can affect your overall statistics. The solution is weeding: the systematic removal of those materials that are out of date, damaged, or simply not checked out enough to justify their existence in our rooms. Determine the use patrons have made of different sections of your library. How often are they checked out? Is the book on free coinage of silver from 1973 in suspiciously mint condition? Take stock of the median publication dates of your nonfiction collection.

How do you balance out reading the newest children's books with the old classics?

The sweatshirt that says, "So many books, so little time," has the correct sentiment. I usually will pick up an old classic that I haven't read before when I see a run on that title and a child tells me that her class is reading it aloud in school, one chapter a day. When the kids can't wait to get to the rest of it and they come searching for it on their own, I realize it's a title I should know, and I'll read it myself.

Ieva Bates, youth services librarian,
Ann Arbor District Library, Michigan

Next, see if there are gaps in your collection. What topics do the local schools assign year after year? Working in my own branch, my coworkers and I like to brace ourselves for the yearly arctic animals assignment given to New York City fourth graders. Once a year troops of children and their parents descend on the library, desperate to find books about, and only about, the ermine or the arctic tern. The first year this happened, we chalked it up as a fluke. This proved to be unwise, however. The next year rolled around, and again we had children desperate for the most obscure creatures and critters native to the Arctic. Do individual teachers always do the same topics year after year? Not necessarily, but it's dangerous to make assumptions. To ascertain the answers, you need to do some outreach. Contact the teachers and school librarians in your area and find out what parts of your collection need beefing up—particularly if you encounter a schoolwide project that is a curriculum staple.

The easiest way to find out what you do not have is to listen to your patrons. When dealing with the public, you're going to find yourself dealing with an offshoot of Murphy's Law: if a topic can be missing from your collection, a topic *will* be missing from your collection. And what's more, your patrons will let you know in no uncertain terms exactly what those items are. To combat this, many libraries keep a list of "needs" at the reference computer, systematically recording every reference question that went unanswered and every title that went unfulfilled. If three people in a single week come in asking for nonfiction titles about Bigfoot, you may want to scout about and find something to satisfy them. Mind you, not every request will even yield a book that's well written and strong enough for the collection. I once had a class of first graders come into the room, and after my presentation about half the class mobbed my desk desperate for books on Mexican wrestlers appropriate for their age and reading level. I was sad to be unable to provide them with that topic, but a search after they left revealed that this is one of those areas where no books are available. Such are the limits of our field.

Your coworkers are also invaluable help. Everyone from the pages to the clerks to the librarians who work in the children's room can be helpful in assessing where your real needs lay. I've found teen pages to be particularly useful when it comes to the latest book in a popular series I don't follow or a title that has spread like wildfire with children the age of their younger siblings. Coworkers who happen to be parents (if you aren't one yourself) also keep on top of the noteworthy trends and school subjects that their own kids have to be able to check out for class.

OLD AWARD WINNERS

Here is a situation you may find yourself in. A parent comes in with a list of award-winning books. She hands you the list and asks that you, the librarian, read through it and tell her which are the most interesting/enlightening/engaging. First, be honest with parents like this. If you do not recognize the books on this list, tell them. Take a look at the school that is handing out the list as well. If it's local and you expect more requests like this in the future, you may wish to ask the parent's permission to copy the handout and do some research on it when you have a chance. If you do recognize the books on the list, you can certainly pull the ones you know of off the shelves. There is a better way, though. The temptation, particularly when it comes to busy or rude parents, is to hand over these books and be done with them. Yet if you are able to speak to the parent at length, this can be a good time to conduct a reference interview. Find out what kind of a reader you're dealing with. Will this child feel comfortable paging through *Johnny Tremain*? Is the child a reluctant reader who would do better with the far shorter *Sarah, Plain and Tall*? Does he or she eschew "boy books" or "girl books"? Find out as much as you can about the child. And if the kid is actually standing in front of you, all the better. Don't be surprised, however, if the parent isn't entirely aware of the child's reading habits. Just find out as much as you can and inform their selections based on the books you think this young patron will enjoy the most.

Becoming entirely familiar with your collection means reading old, dusty stuff. Sorry, but there's no getting around it. You may love the crisp cover and pure white pages of the newest books, but that's going to do you very little good when a parent stands at your desk demanding that you explain the different between *Waterless Mountain* and *Dobry*. So where do you begin? The best place might be among children's books that have been receiving prestigious awards for the better part of the past century. All you have to do is read through them and determine which ones are still pertinent to today's children. With an eye to your audience, read through old lists of award winners and identify the ones that your young patrons will enjoy.

The top two awards known and loved by professionals in the children's literary field are the Newbery and Caldecott Medals. When I took my first children's literature classes in the master's program at the College of St. Catherine, I was astonished, even stunned, when my professor announced that she had been on a Newbery committee and had helped to determine the award. It seemed so wonderful to be a part of an award that has lasted more than eighty years without interruption.

The Newbery Medal was the creation of a publisher and editor rather than a librarian. Frederic G. Melcher was the editor of *Publisher's Weekly* when, in 1921 at the ALA annual conference, he announced the creation of an annual award for "the most distinguished contribution to American literature for children." At first, the winners and runners-up were chosen by popular vote, but after three years of this, the medal shifted to committees. In 1937 the Caldecott Medal, for most distinguished American picture book, was established and was decided by the same committee members, remaining that way until 1978, when they were split into separate committees.

I once made the choice of reading the Newbery Medal winners from old to new. It seemed like a fun activity to try, though locating some of the older titles proved a challenge. As I read, I discovered interesting things about the winners. For example, the 1936, 1937, and 1939 winners (*Caddie Woodlawn*, *Roller Skates*, and *Thimble Summer*, respectively) all featured headstrong tomboys, though only one book ended with the girl still acting that way. And 1935's *Dobry* and 1932's *Waterless Mountain* both featured boys who wanted to become artists, though from two very different perspectives. It soon became apparent to me, however, that not all Newbery and Caldecott Medal books are created equal. Around 1949 I bogged down and never returned to my Newbery reading. My score today is a lamentable fifty-three (one I hope to improve someday).

Some librarians may also like to try their hand at reading through all the Newbery Medal winners they can, starting with the oldest and working their way to the newest. Fortunately, this is not a requirement of the job (phew!). Reading the older titles can be difficult. None of this is to say that there aren't some great books out there, of course. *99 Balloons* and *Strawberry Girl*, for example, remain memorable additions to any children's collection, and for good reason. You must find a way to sort through and extricate the good award winners from the bad so as to recommend the ones that have stood the test of time.

As I read through a variety of these older books, I found myself loving some of the stories while seriously disliking others with an unaccountable passion. We all have books that we don't much care for in our collections. The important thing to remember here, however, is balance. I definitely feel that the 1938 winner, Kate Seredy's *The White Stag*, a story about Attila the Hun, is one of the most inane, ridiculous, and downright tawdry books I've ever had the misfortune to set eyes on, but if I understand that the book is going to get a lot of requests and fills a need in the community (perhaps the children have a unit on the Huns every year), then I will have to consider selecting it just the same. Always assuming that the book is still in print, of course. If the books aren't, that renders this entire problem moot.

Another point to keep in mind when reading old award winners: many of these titles now appear dated. The important thing is to determine whether the book has any redeeming characteristics. Walter Edmonds's *The Matchlock Gun* may strike you as containing an inappropriate story about American Indians, but what do you tell the parent who insists that it was his or her favorite book as a child? Is *Caddie Woodlawn* racist because of its attitudes toward Native Americans? How about Robert Lawson's *They Were Strong and Good*? Does the sweet story about the author's ancestors sufficiently counteract the book's take on slavery and (again) Native Americans? Sometimes the outdated attitudes are the whole point of having the book in the collection in the first place. I once had a steady stream of graduate students enter my library, hell-bent on finding as many racist and sexist children's books as they could so as to fulfill a literary assignment.

Do you believe in promoting the classics of children's lit? Do you actually promote them? Is there any particular way in which you do so?

I am the ultimate promoter of classics, with and without the quotation marks. I think the best way was to talk to the kids, find out what they liked (in life, if not in books). I'd walk through the stacks with them (or with their parents, if the kids were not there) and pull out a bunch of likely suspects. When the kids were there, I did brief booktalks and suggested they read a page or two. I loved talking to teachers and getting them hooked on books. I also liked looking over school suggested reading lists with students and matching them up with the titles I thought they'd like best. The best situations were when I really knew the children—sometimes from infancy on up—and selected books with them in mind, and we talked about books together. The older classics won't work for everyone, but, boy, have I a created a bunch of Betsy-Tacy fans over the years, and Sydney Taylor, and lots of others. I was honest about the books—some of them are challenging—but I let them know how wonderful I thought the books were.

Carla Kozak, San Francisco Public Library

And this raises the question of whether you should automatically add all the Newbery and Caldecott winners to your collection. Another way of saying this is to ask, Does historical significance trump quality? Not at all. And for all that they won big awards, not all award winners deserve space on your shelf. Is there a good reason to have the 1940 Newbery Medal winner *Daniel Boone,* by James Daugherty, even though you find it an unfortunate product of its time? You should consider the size and scope of your collection. Are a lot of children and parents in your branch looking for award winners? If so, are there enough of these titles that you like that you can do away with the ones that do not circulate and aren't particularly good anyway? Consider whether there is an advantage to collecting and keeping everything. And as you read through them, apply the same set of standards to these books that you would a new title on the marketplace. There are plenty of wonderful old award winners to crowd out the ones that are dull or dated.

THE CLASSICS OF THE NON-AWARD-WINNING VARIETY

So what exactly are classic children's titles anyway, and why are they different from award winners? A classic is any book that has stood, and will continue to stand, the test of time, whether or not it has an award. In practical librarian terms, a classic can also be defined as any book that has existed for twenty years or more in a collection and, due to use, has escaped a librarian's tendency to weed. If a book can remain important or popular in spite of its age, there must be a reason that it continues to exist in a library collection. Determining a contemporary book with classic potential is risky, so let's begin instead with older books that are considered worthwhile reading. In *First Adventures in Reading,* author and literary critic May Lamberton Becker devotes a chapter to locating good classic literature for children. She points out that many of us want to confer on our own children those books that we remember as being important in our own childhoods. Many won't be as beloved by our children as they were by us, which is to be expected. Said Becker on the subject, "There is no point in expecting our children to take over our childhood; they are living busily in their own" (1936, 118). This advice still rings true, despite the fact that it was given in 1936.

The best way to locate classics is to find recommended reading lists, which have been vetted by librarians and other professionals in the field.

Consider superstar librarian Nancy Pearl's *Book Crush* for a spot-on collection of classic titles separated into 118 lists. A little older but no less important is *Choosing Books for Children: A Commonsense Guide* by Betsy Hearne, which was reissued in 1999. Editor and publisher Anita Silvey knows her stuff in her handy guide, *100 Best Books for Children,* and educator Judy Freeman consistently creates great titles and reading lists with her *Books Kids Will Sit Still For* and its sequels. These are just a couple of examples, so there is no need to start from scratch when you're searching for some great classic fare. Rest assured that there are professionals who have already done the hard work for you. The only thing to determine is which ones you trust the most.

You can find classics in public library branches throughout the country. Becker's definition serves our purposes well: "A 'child's book' was one meant to be read by children and offered to them for that purpose, while a 'children's classic' was a child's book that had been repeatedly re-read, and was likely to continue to be re-read, not only by the same child but by successive generations of children" (1936, 120). There is a possibility that some newer libraries will fail to purchase classics when they open new branches with new collections. The hope, though, is that the needs of the community (to say nothing of school reading lists) will convince the materials specialists of the importance of carrying a copy of *Treasure Island* as well as *Harry Potter and the Sorcerer's Stone.*

There are two kinds of classics to include in your collection. As Helen Nesbitt once commented, "Some classics, and also some standards, have the power of immediate and wide appeal, and that others will need slow and skillful introduction" (1956, 27). Classics fall into two distinct categories. First, there are the books that are still fun for kids to read without noticing or caring about their publication date. Roald Dahl can now be considered a classic author, and his books have the advantage of maintaining wide, almost unnatural, appeal with

> The powerful cultural role of children's literature cannot be denied: its classics and best sellers have been absorbed into our bloodstream; they are cherished, revisited, and shared like secret toys and secret loves. Its folk and fairy tales have powerfully influenced our ways of thinking and talking about the human mind and social relations. . . . Children's literature is life-enhancing, life-changing, and profoundly influential; it provides a new lens with which to see the world.
>
> *Jack Zipes (2005, xxxi–xxxii)*

each successive generation of readers. Similarly, the books of Edward Eager can surprise you by reaching out to all children. One of the most memorable class visits my library ever experienced was when a class of third graders came in and, while browsing, one of them was heard to say, "Oh, snap! Edward Eager!" Suddenly the entire class of kids, who might normally be pulling out one another's hair for Captain Underpants or Goosebumps, was fighting to grab what scant Edward Eager books we had on our shelves. A teacher allayed some of my confusion by explaining that they were reading Eager in their classroom. Clearly, these kinds of classics suck kids in with little or no effort on the librarian's part.

And then there are the titles that are beloved of older readers but need slow and skillful introduction to reach today's children. One of the more depressing sights is when a parent walks in with a reluctant reader, determined to "make" a child enjoy *Treasure Island* for the very first time. *Treasure Island, Little Women,* and other wordy classics can certainly be loved and adored by kids today, but they should not be forced on kids who aren't ready to take them on by themselves yet.

The advantage of knowing your classics comes when a parent approaches you with the hope of finding something "good" for a child. In this case, the "good" that the parent is looking for means "old." There are times when the only books parents want are the ones they remember from their own childhood. Their offspring, however, may prefer new books on new paper, like their friends at school are reading. In cases such as these, a reprinted title can be a librarian's best friend. Always keep an eye out for classics that have been recently reprinted in paperback editions or with entirely new illustrators. Children who already love the picture books of Lauren Child will be that much more inclined to pick up her reillustrated edition of *Pippi Longstocking,* just so long as you know to tell them about it.

THE DREADED READING LIST

There are times when a child or parent walks into your library with a suggested reading list from school, and the child has to pick three or four titles from the recommended books. When this occurs, the patron wants the best from that selection, and you are the one best suited to help out. In cases such as this, it will help you to be familiar enough with the standard classics to determine which ones are best for this particular child. I'll be the first to admit that nothing quite sucks the fun out of a book like an assignment, but fortunately there are enough fun and fantastic classics available to ensure that a child acquires a love of reading. Getting to know which of those titles are funny, meaningful, shocking, or sublime will make you an expert in the field of children's literature. Getting to know the classics as well as the contemporary hits makes you a star in the field of children's librarianship. Best of all, it gives you the tools you need to infuse the children around you with a passion and a drive for reading, no matter what the subject area. It's up to you to take the initiative and learn as much as you can about your collection. Remember that though the size, scope, and content of a public children's library change from place to place, knowing your own collection inside and outside benefits both you and the public.

FINDING THE NEW

You can't read every new book. You can try, but there are only so many hours in the day. That means relying on other people to tell you what to purchase. You, as a librarian, must therefore figure out who or what you want to place your trust in. In the old days, a children's librarian located books through three primary methods: professional reviews, award winners, and word-of-mouth. To some extent, this is still true. It's just that "word-of-mouth" has taken on computerized characteristics that our librarian forebears could never have foreseen.

New Award Winners

I always say that trying to predict the Newbery or Caldecott Medal winner in any given year is a terrible bet. The odds are not in your favor. Why? Because when it comes to determining the books currently on bookstore shelves that will someday be designated as classics, the first thing you learn is that you know nothing at all.

Look for awards that go beyond the norm when seeking out good books. Does your collection have enough strong nonfiction and foreign-language translations? If not, then take a look at the winners of the Sibert Award and the Batchelder Award. The Sibert considers the most distinguished informational book. The Batchelder goes to the publisher of the most outstanding book translated into English from a title written in a foreign language in a foreign country. You will certainly want to consider the awards given by groups other than the American Library Association as well. Many states have their own children's awards (the Texas Bluebonnets, the Garden State Children's Book Awards, and others) as do a few literary organizations. Many times a state's library association will award an author or illustrator who is a resident of that particular state an award for his or her contributions, making this an invaluable resource for anyone looking to find hidden gems by local authors. Some awards will fit your library system better than others. Would you like to have more children's titles relating to the Jewish experience? The Association of Jewish Libraries gives out the Sydney Taylor Book Award annually.

There are new awards to look at for great books too. In 1996 the National Book Award added a "Young People's Literature" category. And as children's literary blogs slowly become increasingly reliable ways of learning about the newest titles, there are now awards like the Cybils, which are narrowed down and judged solely by panels of children's literary bloggers. These awards are sometimes so new that they are not yet well known enough to count for much in the eyes of classically trained librarians. Yet it is important to remember that just as there are reliable resources to fall back on, new ones crop up all the time, hoping to gain some legitimacy in the eyes of the establishment. And although your initial reaction may be to scoff at them, I've little doubt that some of these sources will become necessary complements to the old guard in the years ahead. Different awards serve different needs and can make for easy collection development choices, depending on how well you trust them.

When it comes to new books for kids, where do you tend to go for recommendations?

First, in the Bay Area we have a group called the Association of Children's Librarians of Northern California (www.bayviews.org), which meets monthly, and we review books. It is my favorite method since I know the person reviewing the book. I also get to see each picture book, easy reader, board book, etc., and seeing the actual book does make a big difference. I also read reviews, of course, and get recommendations from kids, parents, and teachers, and we even buy "junk food" if people ask for it. I also belong to the PUBYAC [electronic mailing list of Public Libraries, Young Adults, and Children], CCBC [electronic mailing list of the Cooperative Children's Book Center], and ALSC [electronic mailing list of the Association for Library Service to Children].

Penny Peck, San Leandro Public Library

Using Sources

Always use a variety of sources to get the best assessment of a title's worth. Just as no two award winners are created equal, no two professional review sources are created equal. Review sources are professional journals or periodicals containing reviews of the latest titles. They are written by librarians and experts in the field and edited before publication. After reading through enough of these publications, you may find that some are not to your taste. Perhaps you find the reviews in *School Library Journal* from librarians across the country a bit too inconsistent in their opinions. Maybe you think *Kirkus* too mean, *Horn Book* too loquacious, and *Booklist* exactly right. Every publication of reviews has its own tenor and voice. The trick is finding the ones you trust the most and then sticking with them. When I reviewed for *Kirkus* and *School Library Journal,* I found that I had to change my tone depending on the publication. For example, *Kirkus* placed a great deal of importance on concentrating entirely on the material before me, while *School Library Journal* preferred that I make an effort to compare my books to previous titles.

It's best to keep updated on all the latest reprinted titles as well. Usually this takes the form of paperback editions. Keeping up with the newest paperback releases and re-releases is sometimes difficult. Not all publishers alert their librarian customers when a new paperback edition of *Mrs. Frisby and the Rats of NIMH* by Robert C. O'Brien hits bookstore shelves. Publications like *Horn Book* can keep you updated on the newest publications, but by and large you'll need to inspect every publisher's catalog of the coming season if you want to know

---

What do you look for in the items you purchase?

Picture books—illustration, choice of words. That's a little bit more personal I think—what one responds to in a picture book. And nonfiction . . . well, now we're very fussy about sourcing. In general, the publishing field is much more careful about sourcing. I don't know that we used to be. I wonder if you looked at old nonfiction books, if they were as careful about attributing every quote, presentation, map, photograph, diagram, and so on. For graphic novels other than *To Dance,* I rely on reviews because I don't have the vision to follow graphic novels that closely. But I use the *School Library Journal* and *Kirkus* reviews and balance them out.

Susan Pine, New York Public Library

what books each is choosing to republish. There are also some publishers like New York Review Books that seek out older titles that have fallen out of copyright and reprint them with lush new bindings. If you trust the publisher, you may want to check out its books, even if you've never heard of *Uncle* by J. P. Martin or *The Bears' Famous Invasion of Sicily* by Dino Buzzati (both recently released by New York Review Books).

With changes afoot, we need to continue to keep ourselves up-to-date on the best books out there. Like our predecessors, we still have reliable review sources to consult when in doubt. In 1956 librarian Helen Nesbitt suggested that librarians use sources like *School Library Journal, Kirkus, Horn Book,* and *Booklist,* publications that continue to provide some of the best reviews of new and upcoming titles.

Other Recommendations

People have always found good books through word-of-mouth. Today is no different. Technology has simply enabled the "word-of-mouth" to be a little easier to hear. I am speaking, of course, of blogs. The term *blog* is a shortened version of the slightly longer *weblog,* which is a user-friendly website that allows its creator the chance to continually update information. It bears some resemblance to an online diary or journal, though it can be used in a professional capacity as well.

I am not an impartial source on this matter, as I have a blog currently housed on the *School Library Journal* website. My experience with blogging has been absolutely wonderful, allowing me a chance to interact with other members in the children's literary community with differing takes and opinions. I truly feel that blogs are a great method of locating and hearing about great titles. Of course, a blog should almost never be your sole method of research into the worthiness of a title. Just as you wouldn't select a book for your collection based solely on a single review, so too must you take a review on a blog with a grain of salt. Think of a blog as a good friend whose opinion you trust. If that person suddenly decides he or she likes a book that you are unfamiliar with, you might take this opinion as a starting point. Now that you've heard about the title, you go forth, locate professional reviews on the subject, and determine whether they're of any use to you. Blogs are a good starting point for discovering books that may not have been properly reviewed in the mainstream press. Select two or three that you trust the opinions of and try to read them every day.

There are other ways to garner information about books, both old and new, but they can be even more suspect than their bloggy brethren. Customer reviews on online websites like Amazon.com and barnesandnoble.com have some use, but they're less reliable than even blogs. I owe much to Amazon since I taught myself how to review by posting thoughts on Amazon. I continue to do so, because I think that Amazon reviews are, for better or for worse, some of the most frequently consulted online. I'm now in the Top 50 Amazon reviewers, which means that my reviews are some of the first that customers see. And although the quality of the opinions on such a site may be mixed, at least you get to read the direct reactions from the people most interested in this kind of literature. On these sites, anyone with a spare minute or two can write in an opinion on a title without being held accountable for it. It's freeing but uncontrolled. With a blog, you get your information from a single source, either one person or a group of people with an interest in children's literature. Online booksellers that allow customer reviews, however, are very hit-and-miss. Sometimes you will stumble on a reviewer who is eloquent and has thought out a response. There are times, however, when you'll encounter customers who wrote the first things that sprouted in their brains after they read a book. There's something to be said for that, of course. And this is one of the few ways in which you can read reviews by children about the books they are reading. Many times a teacher will assign a class to review a book on an online site. And if the kids aren't afraid of saying what they truly feel, you can get a clear sense of what they really think about a book.

PUBLISHING

A library's mission statement, educated librarians, and an outstanding variegated collection guide its purchasing hand. We also need to remember that our work is affected by what's available. A librarian can fill gaps or holes in a collection's subject matter only if publishers are willing to put out books on those topics. We have more choices today than ever before. Unfortunately, sometimes we cannot fill a need because a publisher has not produced any information on a topic.

Consider too that the world of publishing changes every three minutes. One minute young adult titles are the hot item, and the next minute picture books are selling like hotcakes. Blink again and now it's 500-page fantasy novels. Youngsters note these changes and tailor their own demands accordingly. It's up to the libraries to keep attuned to what children want and to make a balance between the hot new genre and other necessary subject areas.

If you can meet with people working in publishing, consider doing so. There is no better way to get a sense of what editors and marketing directors think young readers want than talking to these people in person. To know what they're thinking is to know how they may shape the desires of child consumers, which is to say *your* potential readers. And by discussing these matters with publishers, you can offer opinions on what children are looking for in books and what kinds of books are needed. The people on the front lines getting children interested in books are not usually publishers but librarians.

Attending conferences is another way to find out how publishers think and what they are going to provide in the future. If you are a member of the American Library Association, you can meet many of them on the conference floor during the midwinter and annual meetings. Publishers are fond of holding breakfasts during ALA conferences that are open to anyone willing to drag themselves out of bed at 7:30 in the morning. Publicists staff tables on conference floors during other meetings as well. You might want to consider attending Book Expo or Comic-Con to get a sense of what's out there. Publishers are there to talk to you and are willing to divulge the newest literary trends and influences.

There's a reason the American Library Association conference is as popular a venue with publishers as it is. Ours is a hugely influential organization, and librarians are courted for a reason. To some extent, our purchasing power on behalf of our library shapes the books that are being published. If we all decide to buy more ninja nonfiction titles, publishers might decide to produce more of the same. Therefore, we

How do you deal with self-published patrons?

I haven't had a self-published author coming in person per se, but once in a while we get an e-mail, snail mail, or phone call from someone selling their book. I tell them I need to see a review and give them the information on how to submit a book to *School Library Journal* for review. I also get people who come in and want me to look at their manuscripts or artwork (for free, mind you), as if I will edit their stuff. I tell them I cannot since I am on an award committee, and we are not allowed to see things before they are published.

Penny Peck, San Leandro Public Library

have all the more reason to find the best books and, through our dollars, persuade the publishers to keep bringing out more of the books we want and need.

PROMOTION FROM THE SOURCE

Consider the following situation. You, the librarian, are sitting peacefully at your reference desk when you are approached by a patron holding a large folder. After complimenting your collection, the person mentions that she is a local author or illustrator who has written a picture book. From the hugely positive response the author has received from her friends and family, it's clear to her that this book is something special. Might she drop off a copy with you for possible inclusion in your collection?

You can learn everything there is to know about the books published in a given season, but there may be one area of publication that will surprise you: no matter where you live, children's books authors and illustrators reside. Even the smallest town may harbor an award-winning author in its midst. Some writers and illustrators who approach you will be big names who have written with big publishers and are known nationwide. More common, however, are the small press or independently published writers and artists. These are people who would love to get their books into your library collection. For many, there is no better feeling than to walk into a library and see a book that you had a hand in sitting there on the shelf. Whether the authors or illustrators you live near are big names or little names, the fact is that you need to be ready to answer them when they hand you their books with the clear intent of having it added to your collection.

A stigma is attached to self-published authors, the thought being that if they couldn't publish professionally, then there must be something wrong with their writing. There is always a temptation to write off every person who comes through the door bearing his or her own titles, and this is not entirely fair. It's possible that a lot of what you'll see firsthand will be dreck. Whether the author is a first-time grandfather or a former beauty queen, there is a widespread assumption that anyone can write a children's book (which explains the plethora of celebrity-penned titles). Inevitably, these people are bolstered by their friends and family who honestly like what they've written. The problem comes when you are asked to ascertain the value of their work. It can be awkward telling someone that even though their family members may love their title, you do not. All the same, it is important to look at every book that comes through your door because there are always hidden gems. Sometimes the smallest publisher produces a book of pure gold.

Sometimes you may find these people to be extremely helpful. Smaller communities may need local authors to write their local history and either self-publish or find a small local press. You may wish to have a section of your library dedicated to local authors. Certain bookstores do this from time to time, and it has proven to be quite popular with residents of the area. Just make sure that no matter how much you need a book to cover a particular subject, you give each title that comes through your door a thorough inspection. When a book is too small to get a professional review, you, the librarian, become its most important judge.

CONCLUSION

Just as there is no single way of finding great books, there is no one way to evaluate them. Whether a book is sent to you in the mail or you find it thanks to a state award, you are the one who will be placing (or not placing) the book in the hands of your patrons. Use your best judgment, and your passion for the specialty will help you navigate the enormous swath of literature.

Overlooked Gems in Novels and Picture Books

Here are a few titles I've always thought deserved more attention. Most of these are out of print, but if you can track down one or two of them I guarantee they'll make your day. Try making your own list of overlooked books from your library's collection in your spare time. One of these books will be the perfect choice for children who complain that they've read "everything."

Novels

The Winged Girl of Knossos by Erick Berry—This forgotten Newbery Honor book would fit in perfectly with the kick-ass girl books of today. Retelling the Icarus myth, Berry weaves together the tale of a girl who can dance with bulls, dive with men, and fly a hang glider when called on to do so. As fun now as it was back in 1929.

Ordinary Jack by Helen Cresswell—Here's where the Bagthorpe series begins, and here is where you should start. No family in the history of the world is as huge, crazy, lovable, and downright insane as this one. Poor Jack.

Black Jack by Leon Garfield—Speaking of Jacks, this one's anything but someone you should pity. It's a tale of an average boy and his escaped, almost-hanged, convict friend. Garfield's delicious language makes this one to read.

Archer's Goon by Diana Wynne Jones—I've a weakness for hired goons, whatever their line of business, and to add the great Diana Wynne Jones to the mix is just the icing on the cake. Funny and breathtakingly original from start to finish.

A Drowned Maiden's Hair: A Melodrama by Laura Amy Schlitz—Because the author won the Newbery Medal, perhaps this book won't remain overlooked. It's a delicious interweaving of mystery, villains, and the kind of plotting that brings to mind *The Secret Garden* and books of that ilk.

Below the Root by Zilpha Keatley Snyder—There are quite a few tales today of kids in strange, seemingly idyllic societies where something nasty and unspoken lurks beneath the niceties of everyday life. This book was one of the first and remains one of the best. And it has kids flying in it.

Picture Books

The Maggie B by Irene Haas—If comfort could be synthesized and pasted between the covers of a book, then what you'd have is Haas and her wonderful tale of a girl, her baby brother, and their ship filled with animals and good things to eat.

Else-Marie and Her Seven Little Daddies by Pija Lindenbaum—A stranger tale than this you may never find, but I do not think anyone has ever identified and defined the idea of unconventional but loving families as well as Lindenbaum. This is the very definition of a book that could never have been originally published in America.

Ultra-Violet Catastrophe! or the Unexpected Walk with Great-Uncle Magnus Pringle by Margaret Mahy, illustrated by Brian Froud—A rambunctious girl finds an unforeseen playmate in her great-uncle. Mud and adventures abound. It's an unexpected tale, to say the least. Delicious language and a very amusing story make this a classic, even if it happens to be a forgotten one.

A Time to Keep by Tasha Tudor—Some people adore Tudor, and others dislike her immensely. I stand firmly in the former category, and this is by far one of her greatest books, one in which the months and seasons come to life under her practiced eye and steady hand.

FOUR

Using Your Materials and Learning from Them

When you work in a library, you're always learning. You learn from your colleagues. You learn from your patrons. You learn when you're shelving materials (overheard in my library: "We have a book called *Cooking the West German Way* for kids?"). When you keep your eyes open and your senses sharp, then each day on the job builds on your already impressive array of knowledge.

Learning is merely half the battle, however. There is also the matter of using the knowledge you've already attained. Many people walk into a public library with a vague sense that its librarians are skilled in every possible subject area. They may be a bit unclear on what exactly a librarian is (something your beleaguered pages and clerks can attest to), but they know that if their children are doing reports on Henry David Thoreau, costumes in ancient Egypt, or just want to read the next hot series, you, the librarian, will know exactly what to recommend.

With an eye to old books and new books alike, it's time to get your favorite titles into the hands of readers. There are multiple ways to do this. Using the physical space of the children's room to your advantage is the first and easiest way to go. You can then promote the books within your professional capacity on the reference desk with child and adult patrons. You can use titles directly with children within storytimes and read-aloud programs. Booktalks provide an ingenious way to engage older children who might otherwise have not heard of or appreciated some of the titles you've come across. Finally, we have other less traditional means of engaging young readers. Sometimes it takes a big event to draw in the crowds and the interest. Using themed events, traveling performers, and author visits are always interesting ways to promote books.

THE PHYSICAL SPACE

Book displays are an art. When you walk into a children's room, your eye should travel to displays of colorful, well-presented books. Some librarians are lucky enough to get large and beautiful renovations to their children's rooms. But most of us have to work with what we have. If you find yourself in a branch library that hasn't seen a renovation since 1965 (and isn't that turquoise tile work *so* appealing?), then you need to do what you can to bring the human eye back to the real star of the show: books.

If you use the physical space of the children's room well, then sometimes the books will sell themselves without relying on you to give a spiel about each and every one. There are several ways to make a room work to your advantage in spite of cracked plaster, ugly drop ceilings, and peeling murals.

First, consider taking a turn around your local bookstore and other library systems to see how they do things. Do they create seasonal or

How do you prefer to jazz up your children's room?

Jazzing up: the usual. Posters. Books on display. The story room had two packed puppet trees. I brought in a lot of my own puppets and toys for storytimes and displays. I also went onto eBay to get a Rowland Lion puppet and an Eric Carle gorilla mother and baby for my colleague Janet. In the various areas I worked in, I did the best I could with what I had to work with. I think the design of children's spaces is getting better and better, and we're getting more support now due to our Every Child Ready to Read initiative, but even in our renovated branches there are space and other limitations.

Carla Kozak, San Francisco Public Library

monthly displays? Displays within a children's room can be as complex or simple as you want to make them. In one branch I worked in, we purchased long yards of police tape with the words "Do Not Cross" and wrapped them around a display of banned books we'd placed on a table of titles. Some people were afraid to cross the tape to look at the books, but for the kids it was like a bowl of tasty, forbidden fruit. Nothing makes a book seem more appealing than to make it appear dangerous. I've seen other displays of banned books in which the books were within hanging cages. On the simpler end of things, you may just wish to keep out seasonal titles in a specific area. If April Fool's Day is coming up, pull every picture book and nonfiction title that might possibly apply. St. Patrick's Day? How many Irish fairy tales are sitting on shelves just waiting to be checked out? Patrons love themes, and they love to pick through similar titles. Such displays are picked over constantly.

In one branch of the New York Public Library system, a librarian had the idea of copying those "staff-recommended pick" notes you sometimes see in video stores or at independent booksellers. Meticulously handwriting each one, she made a display of her favorite books, both old and new, and stuck into each one a slip that covered the plot and the elements of the book that she liked. The idea was a huge success. Adults liked the system because they were able to get instant information about titles without the messiness of human interaction. Kids liked the slips and begged to use them as bookmarks. The librarian obligingly allowed them to do this, which was rather clever on her part. After all, if the kids showed the slips to their friends, then their friends might become interested in reading the books as well. The fact that the notes were handwritten was a personal touch that appealed particularly in this electronic age. Of course, the one flaw with this program is that unless you have multiple copies of several titles, you may find yourself scrambling to replace checked-out books. Librarians may wish to consider recruiting other staff members into writing out their own "staff picks." Also, pages who spend their days shelving might leap at the chance to write out book recommendations of the very titles they put on the shelves day in and day out.

Displays don't have to be relegated solely to your children's room either. If you have access to a front window of your library, ask to have a space reserved for a monthly children's window display.

You are limited only by your time and energy. Your time and energy, however, are probably going to be focused primarily on what the patrons want. Even faster than suggesting books to folks around the room is a good old-fashioned one-on-one personal recommendation. They just don't happen to be quite as easy as creating displays.

REFERENCE AND READERS' ADVISORY

The children entering our libraries today are savvier, more knowledgeable, and (in a sense) smarter than kids in the past. They know which computer games they want to play and the websites that provide them. They use a wide variety of handheld devices to keep in constant touch with their friends and acquaintances. Many of them are latchkey kids. Some see the library as a source of free Internet computer time and not much else. This isn't a bad thing, but if you want to get kids reading books, you need to be creative. In a sense, you must surprise them. In the past, children had no recourse but the library for all their information needs. As librarians Charles Anderson and Peter Sprenkle asked, "Will these children have the faith that today's adults do in the library as the ultimate source for everything?" (2006, 27). It sounds obvious to most of us, but you must sell the library to kids from diapers on up, and one of the best places to do this is at the reference desk.

Basic Considerations for Conducting Reference Interviews with Kids

- The student may not know what to expect, or the precise reaction the [librarian] will have to the question.

- The average student may have no pre-knowledge of the type of resource(s) that will answer his or her question.

- The student's communications skills may not be as refined as the [librarian's].

- The student may not know the terminology (library lingo) used in the reference interview.

- The student may not specifically know what he or she is searching for, due to lack of knowledge concerning the subject or the particular assignment.

- The student may misinterpret the [librarian's] nonverbal and verbal cues.

- The student may be fearful of the [librarian] and certain technologies or frustrated about the question being raised.

Ann Riedling (2005, 92–93)

Reference Questions

The librarian who holds down the fort at the reference desk must deal with two different kinds of questions while there: reference questions and readers' advisory service. Reference questions and transactions are generally the result of compulsory assignments and homework. Readers' advisory covers everything else. Neither is any more important than the other. They simply require that you operate different parts of your brain.

Reference interviews require that a librarian "determine efficiently and productively the nature, quantity, and level of information the student requires, as well as the most appropriate format" (Riedling 2005, 91). As children get older, the bulk of these reference transactions are obligatory rather than optional. Child patrons differ from adult patrons partly because they still need to understand how the library system itself works. As Amy S. Pattee, an assistant professor in the graduate school of Library and Information Science at Simmons College, puts it, "Children's reference services involve not only specialized interviewing techniques but also library orientation and bibliographic instruction" (2008, 30). Many public librarians present library orientation programs to visiting classes or go into schools to teach children how to use library services. One-on-one orientation is perhaps the most effective method of education, however, and requires a basic knowledge of how the young child's mind thinks.

Reference work done directly with children is a particularly slippery interaction, particularly when the child is no higher than your knee.

How important is it to know your collection?

I think it's important to know as many of the books in one's collection as one can, and it's important to learn as much as one can about the child and what he or she might be open to. Some kids are more challenging than others, but I kind of like a challenge. I get pretty enthusiastic about books I love. I've also learned to let the books work their magic. I like to wander around the shelves with child patrons, pulling books out, telling them a little about them. When my head goes blank, it helps to see the books on the shelves. On my best days, I figure out a way to find the book that works as bait and hook those child patrons. We have the best job in the world.

Carla Kozak, San Francisco Public Library

In a large room, small children may understand the purpose of the librarian and seek one out for counsel but will have some difficulty expressing exactly what it is that they want. If they want "the blue book," your reference interview skills must be particularly sharp to figure out exactly which blue book they mean. Generally two- through seven-year-olds see the world in terms of themselves. They "think that everyone experiences the world in the way that they do" (Bishop and Salveggi 2001, 355) and as a result don't think to make their questions particularly adult friendly, that is, questions phrased in a manner that adults can readily understand and comprehend. I've seen more than one librarian listen patiently to a child's extended request only to start glancing around the room wildly for the parent or caregiver so as to come up with some sort of an explanation.

In his article "Reference Interviews: Strategies for Children," Melvin Burton writes a wonderful example of this situation but shows how older children can be just as confusing as younger ones:

> A sixth grader and parent had entered the public library and asked for a book on the "carnivorous forest." Both nodded when asked if what they wanted was a place where plants like the Venus Fly-trap grow. When the boy indicated, "Maybe, but I think it's in Canada," the real question became apparent. What they needed was information on cone-bearing trees of "coniferous forests." A best-seller of several years ago, *Men Are from Mars, Women Are from Venus* by John Gray, discussed the communication between genders as happening from two different viewpoints. Likewise, we could very well ask what planet we are on and what planet the child is on as we experience reference interviews with children. (1998, 110)

Older children (ages seven through ten) are beginning to understand how adults organize their questions. This is great except that the result may be that the children will "complicate [their] question unnecessarily" (Bishop and Salveggi 2001, 356), as the example with *carnivorous* versus *coniferous* shows. And in answering the question of a child of this age, whether it's motivated by his or her own curiosity or a school assignment, it is important to impart some knowledge of how the library works rather than just providing a quick answer without any interaction. To do this, I highly recommend consulting Michael Sullivan's *Fundamentals of Children's Services,* which specifies that the goal of the reference interview is "not just to discover what is the true nature of the question but also to understand what is required to provide an acceptable answer" (2005, 89). Also consider Pattee's (2008) piece on adapting Donna Ogle's KWL method to library service. By determining right from the start what it is that children already *know,* what they *want* to know, and what they've *learned* (the KWL) from the reference transaction, even the most straightforward reference transaction takes on a greater significance with the potential to teach.

So how do you deal with each question on a practical level? A whole host of techniques and styles go hand in hand with the art. You may prefer to interact with the child rather than the adult. Or perhaps you'd like to hearken back to David Maxfield's 1954 advice and provide "acceptance, understanding, communication, and collaboration" (Jennerich and Jennerich 1987, 2). Seek out titles on the topic and see what works best for you. And if your library offers workshops on reference interviews, it's always a good idea to go in for a brushup once in a while. Our skills don't rust, but they can get a little tarnished over time.

Readers' Advisory

Readers' advisory is a different matter altogether. Definitions of *readers' advisory* vary, but the best way to describe it is to say that it touches on needs that aren't strictly defined by research and reference. Readers' advisory helps people discover who they are and what they are interested in. In other words, the questions that weren't handed to the child by a teacher but are things that this child wants to know personally. Virginia Walter has a different take, considering the act of readers' advisory an "art": "Children's readers' advisory depends on far more than adult readers' advisory on 'knowing the books.' Adult services librarians are far more likely than children's librarians to rely on access tools for their recommendations to adults. Children's librarians access their own memory banks and use their intimate knowledge of books themselves when making connections between a child's often unspoken desire or need and the book that will suit" (Salvadore 2001, 43). It is not enough to listen to what the child says that he or she wants. You need to also figure out what the child may *actually* want too. Such questions make for the hardest and most fun you will ever answer. They represent your chance to use your own knowledge while helping a young patron find just the right book.

A young boy walks up to you and wants a recommendation. Immediately your clock is ticking. You need to get him interested in a book, and you need to do it *fast*! Lose the moment, lose the child. If he had his way, he'd probably prefer that you reach under your desk and pluck out the world's most perfect book for him right then and there. This, of course, is not an option unless you have somehow managed to read the mind of the child and figure out precisely what it is he is looking for (a skill our MLIS programs have yet to fully perfect).

The first thing to do is to consider your attitude. How you respond to his question is going to be the difference between merely skimming the child's request and delving into it fully. As Ann Riedling said in her book, *Reference Skills for the School Library Media Specialist,* the way you react to a question "sets the mood for the entire transaction" (2005, 92). You are an authority figure, and maybe a scary one, in this situation. You fall squarely into the realm of the adult, and even the most self-possessed child is going to be put off by anything but an open, thoughtful response. With that in mind, pay close attention to what your young patron is looking for. Make eye contact and ask questions to clarify what it is that he wants. Sometimes it takes several questions to get at the heart of the matter. After a ten-year-old asks for "a good book,"

When you have a favorite older title and you want to get a child to read it, what has worked as the most effective strategy for you?

Subterfuge.

First and most important, it must not look old. Whenever a good new cover comes out, I buy it—even if I'm still keeping the older one—specifically because of the out-of-print issue. When it goes out of print, I want to have options. We invest heavily in Mylar covers. I used to repair covers as a shelver, in fact—there are easy ways to make them last and look fresh. Your menders will already know this trick: Keep a small stash of scraps of various colored paper. Your covers go bad at the top of the spine. Reinforce with a slip of similarly colored paper taped to the inside and put a new plastic cover and label on it.

Second, I try to never offer a child a single selection. Children need to be able to choose for themselves. Parents have a stigma attached to anything they offer their child—it doesn't matter how they offer it. Librarians walk a fine line in avoiding that same stigma. So approach the child the way you would like to be approached when you're shopping: helpful and informative but not pushy. I try to always offer three or four play a game of twenty questions with him to determine exactly what it is that he wants.

The most important thing to do when recommending a book is to speak to its appeal. After all, so much of book recommendation comes down to articulating how a book makes you feel when you read it. Maybe this is why booktalks are such an effective tool with children. When you have a captive audience with a seemingly infinite amount of time (though you'd probably never go above five minutes), you can draw them a picture and truly give them a sense of how the book "feels." When you're doing readers' advisory, however, you can't indulge in the same way. It's not feasible to launch into an extended booktalk every time someone wants a recommendation, particularly if you're dealing with a child under the age of nine. The best thing to do is to work on your descriptive process.

Ideally a librarian could walk a child reader up to the library's stacks, plucking possible titles off and describing them in detail. The librarian would be able to conjure up just the right words and images to draw in the child. It's a skill set that few of us are born with, certainly, and the

titles: enough selection without being overwhelming. I try to be equally enthusiastic about each, yet not over the top and not judgmental. The more you press, the less likely a child is to take your suggestion—at least until you've built a rapport with that child.

In the case when you have known a child for years and you want them to read something particular, bribery works just as well. Tell these children you'll let them do something fun like change the date stamp. (Even though we don't date-stamp anymore, we keep one around for situations just like these.)

I've also tried to create displays specifically around a single book. When the Sylvia Engdahl reissues came out, I was so excited about the new covers I put up a sci-fi/fantasy display . . . the key being to have a mix of things you know will move in the display. Garth Nix, J. K. Rowling, Tamora Pierce, Diana Wynne Jones all went into the display. Guess what? The Engdahl still hardly moved. Sometimes you just have to break your own heart in the job and realize that it doesn't matter. What does matter is that you provide a good selection and that people check out books.

Nina Lindsay, management librarian, children's collection, Oakland Public Library; California, and chair of the Newbery and Sibert Award committees amount of energy a librarian sometimes puts into selling a novel could fool you into thinking that we were booksellers rather than librarians. The skeptical child isn't going to buy the material, but you do need to make it worth their while. And the only way to do that is to make the title sound appealing. As a result, authors Joyce Saricks and Nancy Brown encourage librarians to work on a book's "appeal elements": "Appeal elements describe more accurately the 'feel' of a book. Appeal elements take us beyond the bare bones provided by subject descriptors and reveal more of the novel's essence" (1997, 36). That's fine when you are dealing with adult patrons, but adapting this style to your child readers takes some effort.

According to Saricks and Brown, the four basic elements of describing any novel are pacing, characterization, story line, and frame (mood, atmosphere, tone, and so on). Is it a fast-paced or thoughtful methodical story? Are the characters realistic or fantastical? What does the storyline consist of, and what are the moments in the book that really pop? What kind of appeal does the book have in terms of tone? Remember too that you're the expert here, and if you say that a book is particularly marvelous, your young readers may be inclined to believe it.

What about classics? Is there a way to get a child interested in those? As Helen Nesbitt said on the topic, "It is not enough to give a child what he wants. He must also be unobtrusively persuaded to want the best books we have" (1956, 27). Easier said than done. To my mind, when it comes to classics, feel out your audience. Don't push too hard. Reluctant readers aren't going to find a book as thick as *Treasure Island* to be their cup of tea. In contrast, the reader who will be intrigued will be someone like a very well-read twelve-year-old I knew who had just finished Philip Pullman's monumentally large His Dark Materials series and wanted other books along those lines.

That's all well and good, but how do you describe nonfiction in a similar way? Some children want to get their hands on certain informational books. Keep yourself informed and up-to-date on all the newest nonfiction texts in your collection so that when you show the child the section he or she is seeking out, you can say a little about the books you know and what they have to recommend themselves.

Few librarians are (or would care to be) human encyclopedias. So there is always going to be a time when a child walks up to you and mentions a book that you have never read or possibly never heard of. If she wants similar recommendations, you need to learn what it is about this book or series that appeals to her. Ask her questions that touch on the elements that really spoke to her personally. What kind of genre was it? How long? What did she like about the writing? Saricks and Brown say, "We want to stress that there is no shame in admitting we have not read a book; we cannot read everything" (1997, 75). You have several courses of action to take. For example, you can consult with other librarians on online discussion lists or look the book up on various book lists and determine what it was about the book that various readers liked.

Your coworkers are another superb source of knowledge. Duncan Smith wrote in *The Readers' Advisor's Companion* that an "assumption that librarians tend to make is that all staff are equal. They are not. Different staff members have different levels of expertise in certain topic areas. They also have different interpersonal gifts and varying professional interests and goals" (2001, 69).

Regardless of the size of your branch, you'll have a finite number of brains to pick when you have a particularly hard request. When the Central Children's Room of New York Public Library was located at the Donnell Branch, I had the unique opportunity to work with four other highly skilled children's librarians, and our knowledge was equally distributed over a range of different topics. The head of the children's room was particularly good at answering difficult reference questions and drawing on sources and texts I knew nothing about. Another librarian specialized in early education and teacher resources, as well as cultivating a blog and an interest in children's music, both historical and contemporary. There was a coworker skilled at recommendations and booktalks and who could single-handedly organize everything from literary cafés to a program where kids could read to dogs. And finally the last librarian in the room worked constantly with the foreign-language children's books and understood better than anyone else the processing and physical aspects of the materials being added to the branch. This abundance of riches meant that no matter what question was thrown at us, most of the time we could at least come up with some kind of an answer to even the most unusual requests. As Saricks and Brown are quick to point out in *Readers' Advisory Service in the Public Library,* "In this era of straitened circumstances, with its emphasis on expensive electronic access to materials and information, it is easy to forget that one of our most useful reference sources is the knowledge of our staff" (1997, 33).

There may come a time when you must recommend a book or an author you personally dislike. It could be from a genre you aren't keen on or a writer you've always loathed. It's always a good idea to speak in vague descriptors in terms of other people: "My coworker swears by this book," or "I understand this author is particularly popular with kids these days," or "If you're looking for celebrity picture books, this one has been on the *New York Times* Bestseller List for weeks." It's important not to fulfill that stereotype of the librarian who sneers at patrons' choices; instead, acknowledge their preferences and try to work with them.

None of this is to say that you have to hide your own opinion, though. When asked for mysteries for kids, I initially point out several titles that I think are particularly good. I then direct the patron's attention to some other books that I may acknowledge I do not like as much but that children often adore. Generally I make this concession only to parents looking for titles for their children. If you inform a child reader that you do not like a book, then (depending on their personality) he may be inclined to take your word as law and avoid the potentially inviting title at all costs. It's important to be able to read (so to speak) your audiences and tailor your responses accordingly. In cases where the child wants a book that you dislike, feel free to also recommend other books that you feel are superior to the ones requested by the patron. A gentle nudge toward a secret favorite or too-little-loved gem could be just what the librarian ordered.

Even though you are a children's librarian, youngsters are only some of the people asking you reference questions. Much of the time you may find yourself facing a parent looking for books for their children's

Can anyone do a storytime?

No matter how poor a singer or performer you feel you are, you'll do a great job as long as you believe in yourself and in what you're doing. Children are exposed to way too much slick, prerecorded entertainment today on the Net, on video, and on TV. When they get to hear a live performance, it's a treat. As a live performer, you can respond to your audience in a way that a prerecorded entertainer never will; you can answer questions and change song lyrics and tell jokes that apply to that child or that group of children. As a librarian gains experience performing with children, he or she learns how to improvise and play around with a story or a song and to have fun.

Walter Minkel, puppeteer, storyteller, website designer,
ukulele player, singer, and assistant manager,
North Village Branch, Austin Public Library, Texas

school assignments. At the Central Children's Room, we also had adult researchers, teachers, authors, illustrators, and other experts in the field who would present us with all kinds of interesting questions. You will also get readers' advisory questions from parents desperate to get their child interested in something other than Captain Underpants.

STORYTIMES

People who decide to get a master's in library and information science with a concentration in children's literature may not anticipate the degree to which that specialty is going to demand showmanship. If you take a course on children's and young adult literature, that is one thing. But the minute you take a course in public librarianship as it pertains to young people, you will learn about two staples in a librarian's repertoire: storytime and storytelling. You need to be able to get up in front of a class of young strangers and engage them using only words and maybe the occasional colorful picture.

Storytimes are the bedrock of a successful children's room. By and large, a library that can attract and maintain a steady storytime audience will see its circulation statistics go up accordingly. They provide learning environments for children, as well as adults, introducing new and familiar rhymes and books to families. Storytimes can help children improve their social skills, encourage repeat visits to the library, and develop good feelings about the library that will last them the rest of their lives.

Storytime occurs under a variety of conditions. Most children's rooms schedule regular storytimes. In my room, we have four regular weekly or biweekly programs: Baby Laptime, Toddler Storytime, Preschool Storytime, and a music program for young children. In addition are weekend storytelling performances by traveling performers or a themed storytime by staff members. On top of that are the stories read to classes of children coming from nearby schools for visits. With this many storytimes you need to know how to engage your audience.

To prepare adequately for storytimes, bulk up on your knowledge of books that read aloud well. Ideally, you need to find a book that has great text and great pictures and also meets the needs of the age group before you. For infants, toddlers, and preschoolers, this means interactive books. Always include a couple that you can sing. For example, *Brown Bear, Brown Bear, What Do You See?* by Bill Martin Jr. (illustrated by Eric Carle) when sung to the tune of "Twinkle, Twinkle, Little Star" makes for a mesmerizing read. Lift-the-flap books also do well with this age level and are particularly good with babies. Look for titles with a lot of repetition and fun sounds to hold the attention of the easily distractible. Children between the ages of four and ten require books with a great story and sound. These will be picture books that are meant to be shared with large groups. Their text can also contain repetition, but the story will be longer and more complex. Classic storytelling motifs appear in the text.

So how do you go about finding books that work for your purposes? If you pluck random picture books off your shelves and then try to read them to large groups, you will find that a picture book format does not always a great read-aloud make. Just because it has thirty-two pages and lots of bright and funny pictures, that doesn't guarantee that the book isn't a snooze-fest when placed before the kiddies. You need to know what to look for in a great read-aloud story. Is the book large enough for a large audience to see? Can you sing the text? Are there pop-up elements to engage younger kids?

Observing other children's librarians conducting successful story-times is a wonderful way to get a sense of varying styles and techniques. It is also a brilliant way to discover new picture books that lend themselves to the storytime experience. If you don't have a library system that provides you with a chance to observe, consider the Internet. I have seen brilliant YouTube videos of storytimes where two grown men have reenacted *Don't Let the Pigeon Drive the Bus* by Mo Willems by handing off the book to one another.

Once you've found the ideal book, make sure that there are plenty of copies of the title in your library system. When I do a toddler program, the book I prefer to use is the long-out-of-print *The Noisy Counting Book* by Susan Schade. I've never seen any other book like it capture the attention of a roomful of toddlers. However, the copy we use for storytimes is unavailable for checkout. The result is that every week, someone asks to check out the story, and every week we have to confess that there aren't any copies available at this time. If you select a book to read, be sure it's something you have lots of copies of. My use of *The Noisy Counting Book* leads to nothing but trouble when parents and caregivers come to me afterward begging to borrow my noncirculating book. Fortunately, titles like *Brown Bear, Brown Bear, What Do You See?* are the kinds of stories parents will want to check out anyway! You can make it easy for them by placing a cart of recommended books by the door on the way out of the room so that they can check them out if they want to.

There is also a temptation to read the same three books over and over again during a storytime. In a way, this can be very comforting for the younger children. It can also be dull as dishwater for you, the performer, or the patrons watching. Consider changing at least one book a month. Look at fellow librarians and bookstores to see what titles work particularly well with small children.

STORYTELLING

Story*telling* is entirely different from story*time.* By and large, storytellers do not use a book to convey a tale to an audience. Instead, they simply stand on a stage and let their words alone weave a story told entirely from memory. Many librarians find this to be a nerve-wracking occurrence, but telling a successful tale is an amazing experience. Everyone has a different style or take on one story or another. Getting kids to learn and enjoy that story is often what makes the job worthwhile.

Here is how we tell tales at my library. Each children's librarian is outfitted with a set of storytelling candles. Before each storytelling session, we light the Story Candle at the front of the room. When the stories are done, everyone will have a chance to blow out the candle and make a wish. Then you tell your tales. They can be grouped together thematically or can simply be your favorites, but above everything else they need to engage your audience in some way.

Finding the best stories that work for you is a skill. Some librarians I know find their stories through picture books. I've seen magnificent productions of obscure but fabulous titles like *The Magic Feather Duster* by Will and Nicolas or *How Chipmunk Got His Stripes* by Joseph Bruchac. Always look for a mix of old classics and new titles for your storytelling. For example, when I discovered the picture book *Little Rooster's Diamond Button* by Margaret Read MacDonald, I knew that it would work perfectly all by itself as a story without a book. *Anansi and the Moss-Covered Rock* by Eric Kimmel makes for a surprisingly good retelling as well.

Generally I prefer to get my stories from storytelling collections. My favorite among these would have to be Margaret Read MacDonald's *Twenty Tellable Tales,* alongside anything else she has written. MacDonald fits my style, and you're bound to find someone who fits yours too. Remember that you're looking for stories that will be easy for you to memorize. I always try to consider those that contain a lot of repetition, as these are sometimes the easiest tales to memorize.

When I work a toddler or a preschooler storytime, I do not tend to care what age the children in the audience are, just so long as they are having a good time. Storytelling is a different matter altogether. If you would like to have a program for children from five to ten years old, the last thing you need is to walk into the room and find it full of babies. If you have a storytelling selection, make it very clear to the parents what age group you prefer. If you've memorized stories for toddlers and want to present to them, that is fine, but be aware that patrons do not always examine age limits on a program all that closely.

BOOKTALKING

A single librarian walks before a class of bored, jaded sixth graders. The librarian looks them over, three books in hand, and within five minutes every child in the room will kill for the books that librarian is holding. Sound impossible? Booktalking is perhaps the greatest innovation in the profession since the notion of children's literature itself. What's more, it's the best way I know of to get kids excited about books and eager to share your love of obscure or unknown titles. Unless the book in question is a television show, a movie, or a phenomenon, children need adults like you to tell them about great titles.

The idea of a booktalk is simple. If movie trailers work for movies, why shouldn't book trailers work for books? In a typical booktalk, a librarian stands before an audience with three to four books. It's always a good idea to mix in at least one nonfiction title with the rest for spice. The librarian then holds up each book and gives the audience a little

Do booktalks work?

Booktalks done in person with the book in hand are the best way to convince a kid to read something. Take a bag of books on a school visit and do short talks for each title. Then sit back and watch the reserve list grow at your library. The booktalks work!

But librarians do have their tricks. One branch librarian favorite is saying, "While we're waiting for your book to come out here from the main library, why don't you try this one?" Or when you go to the shelf in search of a specific title, you can pull off some nearby and use your booktalking skills to sell those as well.

Ieva Bates, Ann Arbor District Library

taste of what it's about. Here is an example of a booktalk I wrote for Audrey Shafer's 2006 title, *The Mailbox:*

> Twelve-year-old Gabe Culligan has had a rough life, but things have evened out really well for him lately. You see, for years Gabe was a foster kid, shuttled from place to place without a home. Then his social worker found his long-lost Uncle Vernon, and things were looking good. Sure, Uncle Vernon's kind of crusty. He has a prosthetic leg and a gruff manner, but it's obvious that he and his nephew get along really well. How was Gabe to know that Vernon had secrets? So one day, Gabe comes home from school to find Uncle Vernon dead on the floor. Well what would you do? You can't blame the kid for not wanting to deal with the situation. The next morning, he goes to school like usual and tries not to think about what to do. And when he gets home, there's a note in the mailbox. On one side it says, "I have a secret." On the other side it says, "Do not be afraid." But when Gabe comes into the house and finds that his uncle's body has disappeared, he is afraid. Very. *The Mailbox* by Audrey Shafer.

The point of a booktalk is not to give away the plot or to make a summary of the book itself. In this booktalk I discussed only the beginning of the novel. Sometimes when you're reading a book, the hook will appear in the first few pages. Other times it won't show up until the end. Always mention the name of the book and the title at the end of your talk; then immediately move on to the next book. It's best if you put off questions until you are done so that nothing interrupts the flow of your talks. Some schools of thought teach you to memorize your own booktalk word for word rather than just making up your talk on the spur of the moment. I favor a more relaxed but similar method. If you know the direction you want your booktalk to take, write it out. Then practice a couple of times. If you flub a word or miss a phrase here or there, it's not the end of the world. Simply get a feel for what it is you're trying to say. If you get the gist of the book's excitement and promise across to your listeners, sometimes that's enough in the end.

When booktalking nonfiction, it's always a good idea to make the books interactive. Ask your audience questions. If you have a new *Guinness World Records,* flag preselected sections that you think will surprise and startle the kids. If instead you want to talk up Halls, Spears, and Young's *Tales of the Cryptids,* ask the kids about their favorite, possibly imaginary creatures, and then show them the colorful photographs as you discuss the book's allure. Nonfiction gives librarians the freedom to drill home the fact that while some stories are no more than made-up words, some books are filled with truths that are stranger than fiction. My nonfiction booktalk of choice is John Fleischman's *Phineas Gage: A Gruesome but True Story of Brain Science*. Few things grab an audience's attention quite as effectively as a long iron pole through the top of a man's skull. A skilled booktalker, of course, can take a biography of Benjamin Franklin or Phillis Wheatley and make it pop and sizzle. It's all in the telling.

One problem that I've sometimes run into when booktalking is that it doesn't work unless you have read the entire book that you're discussing and recommending to your audience. If you attempt to fudge your way through a book that you've never read or that you read a long time ago and can't remember well, you won't sound compelling. I once had a class of sixth graders coming to my library, and I wanted them to take a gander of Margaret Mahy's *The Changeover*. Inexplicably my library had somehow ended up with eight or nine copies of the book, and I was eager to get it circulating. I remembered bits and pieces of the plot, but it wasn't enough to get me to recommend the book as well as I might have. One boy, bless his heart, picked it up when I was done, but I know that if I'd simply taken the time to reread the book and give it some thought, others would have followed his lead.

Booktalked books can be old or new titles, though I recommend talking up titles that are plentiful and available in your library system. There isn't much point in getting children excited about *Anna to the Infinite Power* by Mildred Ames if the book is out of print and you haven't a single circulating copy. If you are visiting a school and booktalking from there, consider checking the school library to see what it does and does not have before choosing the titles to talk up. Some Newbery Medal and Honor books make great booktalks, just as long as you can find the hook. It's there somewhere; you just need to know how to bring it to light. Will you talk up *Holes* by Louis Sachar with Stanley Yelnats finding the buried trunk with his name on it? Or *The Higher Power of Lucky* by Susan Patron with Lucky heading out, alone, into a dust storm? And it is inevitable that sometimes you'll start a booktalk and encounter a sea of rolling eyes from children who have already read and reread the book you hold in your hands. Don't let it get to you. Great booktalks can get kids to suddenly want to reread an old favorite all over again. Never forget that your booktalks are not introducing just kids to little-known titles but their teachers as well—teachers who may grow to read, love, and assign these books in the future and maybe help them become part of the literary canon.

Booktalking can exist in venues other than class visits. I run a homeschooler book group out of my library branch, and inevitably the question of what to read next will come up. Often I present three potential titles to the kids, and to aid them in voting for the next book I will booktalk the choices. Booktalking also comes in handy when parents and kids come to your reference desk asking for recommendations. If you already have a prepared spiel in place for a wide array of books, you'll find it easier to convince your patrons of that book's pros and cons than if you simply read them the book flap.

Not everyone takes to booktalking. Most librarians suffer stage fright to various degrees. Considering how nerve-wracking it can be to stand in front of a group of kids with the intent of engaging them, you should always remember that as you do more and more booktalking, it will come more easily to you. That's small comfort the first time you step in front of a group, but there's nothing like seeing kids scrambling to grab the books you've talked up or, if you're visiting a school, frantically writing down the title and authors to put your heart at ease.

Some people can present booktalks without difficulty but find it hard to write their own. When this happens, sometimes it's useful to see written booktalks, which will give you a sense of other booktalkers' styles. Some libraries compile booktalks on their websites. At New York Public Library, this website is viewable only by children's and teen librarians. In Oregon's Multnomah County system, it is available to the public and easy to search. Librarians within their own systems like to trade favorite booktalks and ideas too. Engage your coworkers for suggestions and recommendations. Sometimes the book you couldn't figure out how to promote becomes the booktalking staple you turn to again and again.

There are also some outstanding books on the subject that you may wish to consult. One is *The Booktalker's Bible: How to Talk about the Books You Love to Any Audience* (2003) by Chapple Langemack. It covers everything from choosing the best books and booktalking to different age groups (even adults) to the Golden Rules of Booktalking. It also helps librarians for whom public speaking is particularly difficult. Sometimes getting help from a professional is the best idea, and Langemack's book is a kind and intelligent read.

PARTY TIME

Everybody likes a party. Heck, everybody likes *to* party. And when it comes to the public, there are few methods more effective than big parties celebrating books. Many library systems already celebrate the end of their summer reading programs with summer reading parties or, as many prefer that they be called, "celebrations." Such events were not always part of what libraries did, but over the years they have grown more common. In the case of New York Public Library, celebrations were directly tied into the promotion of the yearly summer reading program. By the end of the 1990s they had become common, and these days they can be used for any event, just so long as it is book related in some way.

Depending on the library system you work in, there may be money in your budget for parties. The difference between a $500 and a $50 celebration is minimal, however, when the right amount of creativity comes into play. For example, two librarians I know decided to do a Clementine event, based on the books by Sara Pennypacker. When Jolie Hamer-Conroy and Kiera Parrott sat down and thought of what to do, they looked at the book and came up with a series of activity stations. Kiera had this to say of them:

> Pin-the-Bologna-Eyeglasses-on-Clementine Game: "This
> worked pretty much like Pin the Tail on the
> Donkey. I originally wanted to use real bologna

What kinds of parties have you done in the library?

I actually used to do extravaganzas. I did a rain program where I read rain stories, and then I put on "Singing in the Rain," and I bought a hula hoop, decorated it in blue, and they had a little platform at Bloomingdale's, it's yea high, and so we jumped into the puddle and splashed. And then we hung crepe paper so we could crawl under the waterfall. Then I did a circus program where we lifted weights (which were made of construction paper) and we walked a tightrope (which was yarn about twelve inches apart on the floor) and that was a lot of fun actually. Oh, and we jumped through a "flaming hoop" (crepe paper on a hoop in flame colors). So I did things like that. And that's when we started parties. When we started the citywide summer reading program.

Susan Pine, New York Public Library

but got talked out of it. I wound up making fake
pieces from construction paper and glue. If I
do this party again, I'm definitely using the real
thing!"

Pigeon War: "I printed color copies of pigeons and
mounted them on pieces of cardboard. I created
little stands for them and arranged the pigeons
on a book cart. The kids had to stand about ten
feet back and, using only three small beanbags,
knock down as many as they could."

Tattoo Station: "This was really just face painting and
temporary tattoos, but we arranged the paints
and designs in such a way as to suggest a tattoo
parlor. Kids got everything from dragons on their
forearms to a full-face Spiderman mask."

Miscellaneous: "We also had a Coloring Station (to serve
as a creative outlet between activities) and a
Decorate-Your-Own-Cupcake Station."

The result was a celebration that a lot of children will never forget,
and it became a great way to get them interested in a book that they
may otherwise never have heard of. Titles that are contemporary and
popular will attract more interest than obscure ones, but the nice thing
about celebrations is that everyone wants to come to one. You may have
food and drink issues that limit what you can hand out, but that doesn't
mean you can't still have a good time. Also consider how large a group
you can accommodate. Kiera and Jolie decided to limit the number of
children to fifty by registering them beforehand. This was possible since
they held much of the celebration in their programming room and could
check off the children as they came in. If you work in a more open space
than this, you may wish to limit your numbers in other ways.

If the celebration is based on a new or recent book, you might also
want to contact the publisher for some promotional materials. Said
Kiera, "Hyperion was nice enough to send a bunch of tabletop stands
and bookmarks, and we used leftover summer reading incentives as
prizes." Authors and illustrators, no matter how important or well
known, also like to hear about celebrations based on their own books.
If you take digital pictures of the event and forward them to the book's
creators, you might even be able to convince them to come to your
library the next time you throw a shindig.

Sometimes libraries base their celebrations and events around specific traveling performers hired by the library to entertain the public. These might include magicians, jugglers, yo-yo enthusiasts, storytellers, puppeteers, and anyone else who can engage an audience and turn the conversation back to books. Performers can be selected, according to their skills, to complement previously existing celebrations, like those celebrating the end of summer reading, as well as holidays and the like. Consider setting up a display of books that relate to your performer that kids might want to read. If you have a magician, pull out all your magic books. If you've a storyteller, ask beforehand what the stories will be and then find books to match. Place this display in a prominent location where kids have to pass it. If you put it to the side of your program, it may look very pretty, but the kids will probably pass it by without casting it so much as a second glance.

And, of course, authors and illustrators are a great tie-in to any library program. Many of these people will have performed in front of crowds and large school groups in the past and will be comfortable talking to children. Find out ahead of time what age range they prefer to speak to. As with all other performers, provide them with glasses or bottles of water, an easel if they need it, pens, a display of their books, and just about anything they need. Sometimes they will also want to be able to sell their own books. Before agreeing to this, find out whether the library allows for-profit sales within its walls.

CONCLUSION

The practical application of child to book is a complex process. I think that one of the things I love the most about librarians is how creative they've become when it comes to introducing children to new titles. You might think that there was only so much you could do, but every day brings a new way to introduce a soon-to-be-beloved title to a child. Remember too that every librarian's style and skill set is different. Maybe you're an engaging storyteller but only a so-so booktalker. Use whatever you have to get kids interested in your collection. Sometimes it's all that you can do.

Great Read-Aloud Picture Books

I get more requests for my favorite picture book read-alouds than any other subject. And to my mind, a good read-aloud is money in the bank. This is my list of surefire storytime hits for the above-four-years-old crowd. Resist them if you can.

Snip Snap, What's That? by Mara Bergman, illustrated by Nick Maland—If you can get the kids to yell all together, "You *bet* they were!" then any reading of this book will be a hit. Even kids a little scared of the alligator will love the silly ending and empowered children.

Fortunately by Remy Charlip—This one makes for fabulous reading. Since every page turn goes from good to bad to good to bad, the kids will enjoy trying to predict how the story turns out.

Bark, George by Jules Feiffer—Few other picture books can delight as many teenagers as they do five-year-olds. The animal sounds will delight the younger set. The Feiffer illustrations, silly premise, and surprise ending will suck in the older kids.

Oh! by Josse Goffin—Another great audience participation title. There aren't many words, so you'll have to do a little banter on your own. Just the same, make sure all the kids go "Oh!" whenever you lift the large flaps that rearrange each seemingly simple image.

The Chicken-Chasing Queen of Lamar County by Janice N. Harrington, illustrations by Shelley Jackson—Delicious language, a spunky protagonist, and art that virtually pops off the page. There is nothing here not to like.

My Lucky Day by Keiko Kasza—As you can probably tell, I'm a huge fan of a good twist ending. Kids love 'em too. And in this story, the fear that the pig will be eaten is completely obliterated by the end of the tale. Besides, how often do you get to read a book in which a pig gets a thorough massage from the story's antagonist?

Footprints in the Snow by Mei Matsuoka—The ultimate unreliable narrator, a hungry wolf, decides that his kin have been getting a bad rap in this charming look at how writing a story can go horribly wrong.

Duck on a Bike by David Shannon—Another animal sound book and another book with a twist ending. Shannon's books always read aloud well because his pictures are easy to see from a distance. This one will blow the kids away.

FIVE

Your Own Time

Right off the bat I want to make it clear that when I talk about working in your free time, it is merely as a suggestion. No librarian should feel obligated to sacrifice time away from work to their job. After all, the last thing I want to do is convince you that you should be at your job twenty-four hours a day, seven days a week, physically, mentally, or in spirit. Everyone needs some downtime. As much fun as it might be, you probably don't want to spend every waking hour reading as many children's books as possible, eschewing your own adult reading in the process.

That said, if you love children's literature as much as I do, then participating in professional development during your off-hours isn't a chore. It's fun! Whether you're trolling the kidlit blogs, taking notes on other library systems, or just visiting your local bookstore, every day can provide a little learning experience. Professional development outside the workplace boils down to anything you do that aids you in your job. And getting a sense of the new things out there, as well as visiting the old things you might not have been aware of, can be useful to you as a professional no matter where you are. Whether you're surfing the Web or visiting libraries in other states, you can keep connected to what's new, what's old, and what's available for public consumption.

WHAT YOU CAN DO AT HOME

Helloooo, World Wide Web.

Time was that the hours spent in your home would be used primarily in reading new and old books. Now the Internet allows us to be tied to communities that share our aims, interests, and aspirations at all hours of the day.

In the early days of the digital age, one of the first methods of online discussion for advocates of children's literature was electronic mailing lists. Subscribers use these lists to receive information by e-mail that is written by many Internet users. Lots of mailing lists pertain to the children's literary aspects of our profession. As of this writing, the PUBYAC discussion list is "concerned with the practical aspects of Children and Young Adult Services in Public Libraries." The CCBC-net electronic mailing list, run by the Cooperative Children's Book Center, focuses monthly on topics of concern related to children's and young adult literature. And one of the first and finest of these electronic mailing lists is child_lit, created by Michael Joseph and run out of Rutgers University. Begun in 1993, the site currently has 2,000 members, and more join every day. The site has become a center for intelligent, ribald discussions of children's literature and features such big-name members as authors Philip Pullman, Jane Yolen, and Julius Lester.

> ### Do you do anything in your spare time to help you become a better librarian?
>
> I would like to think so. Because I'm a school librarian, I've found that the best way to improve my work is to get to know my children better. I've sometimes joined them by sharing their writing or art assignments. I've made things with them—watercolor pictures, or calendar books, or origami dragons. I've helped them rehearse plays, played with them at recess, or gone sledding with them. It all sounds like I'm goofing off—having much too good a time—but joining them in their world strengthens the bond between us. The time I've spent working and playing with my school-children is more fruitful than any conference I've ever attended or any packet of information I've ever read.
>
> *Laura Amy Schlitz, librarian, Park School, Baltimore,*
> *and a Newbery Medal winner for her book* Good Masters!
> Sweet Ladies! Voices from a Medieval Village *(Candlewick, 2007)*

Electronic mailing lists still provide some of the best ways to listen in on conversations about children's literature. Subscribers who read others' conversations but do not contribute themselves are called "lurkers." In terms of keeping up with the profession, lurking can be a productive way to keep a finger firmly on the pulse of the current children's literary debate. But it is not the only method of online conversation available.

Social networking services came after electronic mailing lists, making use of websites rather than e-mail. Such sites create online communities of people with common interests, enabling them to participate in some kind of a dialogue. Popular social sites like Facebook and MySpace eventually inspired book-based equivalents, which took on lives of their own. These book-related websites include Shelfari, LibraryThing, and Goodreads, and more are cropping up every day. Users are encouraged to update the books currently on their shelves, rate them, and discuss them in online groups with other like-minded individuals. Such participation can easily take quite a bit of time out of your day. But rather than view these increasingly addictive sites as a time suck, consider using them for your job. I've often found that Goodreads can give me insightful views of forthcoming books because of the sheer number of booksellers that contribute to the site. Booksellers often see advanced reader copies of titles long before their librarian fellows do. Finding their opinions on children's books aside from blurbs on upcoming titles has proved difficult in the past. Now, thanks to online social groups, it's becoming easier and easier to find literate, thoughtful responses to books long before their publication dates. Another use of these sites is to "friend" your patrons. If patrons in your library trust your opinions and want to see what you're currently reading, you can advise them to befriend you on one of these online sites, providing for their needs without consistently having to e-mail them individually.

Another way of using the Internet to engage in professional development is to consider joining an online group. Google, Yahoo!, and other sites may provide Internet communities that offer instant connection with people who share your interests. The downside is that the readership on these kinds of sites, if they are open to the public, can be hit-or-miss. They can also be difficult to locate without an invitation. If you don't see what you're looking for, start your own group and encourage others to join.

Finally, there's nothing finer than getting information from professional organizations for free. Periodicals like *Horn Book, School Library Journal,* and *Publishers' Weekly* have found that subscribers to their print publications appreciate receiving updates and news in an e-mailed newsletter format. By subscribing to their newsletters, you may receive access to podcasts, additional reviews, and the latest information. Free online articles are also available when the publication can get enough money from its ad revenue to justify offering text for free. A rainy Sunday can become instantly productive when you have *Horn Book* archives to read through.

WHAT YOU CAN DO OUT AND ABOUT

Every time you leave your house, you leave yourself wide open to potential children's literary experiences. I'm often amazed how often the world of children's literature presents itself to the average adult. That ride on public transportation can prove particularly fruitful if you observe other people's children and their reading choices. Similarly, a jaunt to the park might yield children's literary characters in the statuary or design.

You don't need to have kids of your own to visit some of the best places that speak to the state of contemporary children's literature. For example, whenever I visit another city or county, I make a point to visit the local library or central branch with an eye toward checking out their children's rooms. There is no more eye-opening experience than seeing how other library systems do it. While visiting my brother-in-law and his wife in Greensboro, North Carolina, I popped into one of the Greensboro libraries and got some great ideas on how to pump up displays. I did the same thing when I visited my sister in Chicago and noted that it shared New York's difficulty in keeping adults off the children's Internet computers.

When you find yourself in an unfamiliar library, grab some fliers and see what they offer. Check out their displays and the books that they think are particularly fine choices. Observe the room layout and how they've dealt with the space that they've been given. Make a note of what works and what doesn't. How do they handle problems that your library branch has encountered? For example, if you have a problem with parents and caregivers doing their e-mail on the children's computers, see if the same problem carries over to other library systems and what they do about it.

There's no better way to get a sense of the room than to strike up a conversation with one of the librarians at the desk. Working the desk at the Central Children's Room of New York Public Library, I was lucky enough to meet librarians from all over the world. Many were interested in our automated computer system, which allowed kids to log in using their library cards. Others wanted to know about the extent of our collection, our purchasing processes, and how long we had been around. Every library system has its own personality, and half the fun of meeting new children's librarians is getting to see them in their natural environment. Better still is seeing how they cope with difficulties that you also have to deal with.

It's important to remember that libraries aren't the sole repositories of books. There is the little matter of bookstores. You don't even have to leave your city to get a sense of these places. In your local bookstores, find out when authors and illustrators for children are coming in to speak and sign their books. If you're in another city, you can do the same with the libraries you visit, but new and upcoming authors sometimes prefer the bookstore circuit and will travel there for a couple of years before being invited to speak at libraries. Also consider staying for a bookstore storytime. Sometimes you can pick up useful tips and tricks from people outside the library profession. The Red Balloon in St. Paul, Minnesota, was recommended to me as a great place to visit for a kicking storytime when I was taking a class in Children's and Young Adult Services while getting my MLIS degree in Minnesota. It's also a great way of finding out what new books (books your library may not have as of yet purchased) make for good read-alouds. Used bookstores can prove to be treasure troves too. Many times I've heard about an old or rare children's title that was uncovered sitting on the shelf of a much overlooked used bookstore.

When visiting major cities (or even those of the small to moderate variety) it can be a lot of fun to go on a children's literary tour, even just a self-guided one. Find out the local places of interest. For major cities like New York, there are helpful guides like Leonard Marcus's *Storied City: A Children's Book Walking-Tour Guide to New York City* (2003). Smaller towns often tend to have their own points of interest, though. Check with the local children's librarian, and you may find that while you're in Littleton, New Hampshire, you can see a statue of Eleanor H. Porter's Pollyanna. Or maybe you'll find yourself in Columbus, Ohio, near the James Thurber House and Museum.

REVIEWING AND WRITING FOR PUBLICATIONS

Reading online conversations or enjoying the sights in cities is fun, but these are particularly passive activities. If you want to add something to the conversation, you will have to add your voice to the chorus.

Reviewing and writing articles allow you to extend your reach. You already recommend books to the people in your immediate sphere. Why not try to increase the number of people who know and trust your opinions?

There are two ways to attack the question of whether to review children's books. Would you like to do so in a professional capacity, influencing the hearts and minds of readers across the country? Or would you perhaps prefer to review in a personal capacity, potentially to a smaller (if more dedicated) readership? The advantage of reviewing professionally is that you are often sent titles and authors you might never see if it were not for your journal's largess. What's more, if you take it upon yourself to read and review books that are already in your collection on a website or blog, you are educating yourself and, in turn, your patrons.

While earning my library degree, I took a children's literature course that covered the idea of reviewing. Part of our class consisted of reading K. T. Horning's *From Cover to Cover,* a book I treasure to this day. Horning's book covered both the theory and the practical matter of reviewing. I read it thoroughly and was so inspired that I thought I might try my own hand at it. Amazon.com, free to the public and viewable to countless eyes, seemed the perfect place to do so. I cut my teeth on reviewing titles there first. It was a good place to start to get a sense of my personal style. In the beginning, my reviews were short and to the point. I indulged in a sentence or two of personal opinion, dedicating the rest of the review to a plot or text summary. Once I'd grown comfortable with my writing, I contacted an online reviewing site that would send me free advance reader copies in exchange for reviews. It didn't pay anything, but that didn't bother me particularly. What did bother me was that the site preferred that all reviews be positive, and

Should librarians review?

I do recommend reviewing, and I get a ton of questions from folks who want to receive free review copies. Start at the local level and build a body of work. Get experience putting your thoughts down on paper in that controlled style. Use it as a way to model good reviewing with your students. The time I have spent thinking critically about literature has helped me to become a better librarian for my students.

Walter M. Mayes, Girls' Middle School, Mountain View, California

the books I was sent were often of less-than-stellar quality. Still, my brief experience gave me the credentials (and confidence) I needed to contact *School Library Journal* (*SLJ*). Like its teen equivalent, *Voices of Young Adults* (*VOYA*), *SLJ* relies on reviews from librarians across the country. To review, you simply apply with some writing samples. *SLJ* does not pay, but after reviewing a book you are sent a hardcover copy as a thank-you. This happens regardless of whether your review was critical or laudatory. *SLJ* provided me with years of great experience; I stopped reviewing for it only when I began to write for *Kirkus* (which paid!) instead.

The idea of a children's librarian reviewing is practically as old as the profession itself. Consider the mother of American children's librarianship, Anne Carroll Moore. The premiere head of children's services at New York Public Library, Moore "probably did more than anyone in those early years [1900 and on] to define and institutional-ize public library services for children" (Walter 2001, 4). What's more, she was a prolific reviewer. "She wrote reviews of children's books for the respected literary journal, *The Bookman,* from 1918 to 1926, and in 1924 she instituted the regular column, 'The Third Owl,' for the *New York Herald Tribune.* She continued the Third Owl tradition and logo in regular contributions to *Horn Book* from 1936 to 1960" (Walter 2001, 5). Reviewing in a professional capacity is infinitely rewarding. Whether you find yourself writing for *Horn Book, Kirkus, VOYA, Booklist, School Library Journal,* or the countless other professional publications, it's wonderful to see your words appear on a book's blurb or advertisement and to know that you were the one responsible. You are reaching an audience of professionals when you review that you might never reach otherwise. It's deeply satisfying.

Reviewing in a personal capacity almost requires a different set of muscles. When I began to review for *School Library Journal,* I never stopped reviewing for Amazon. Naturally I would never review the same book in a professional and personal capacity (books reviewed for journals were never reviewed online), but I found a satisfaction with my Amazon reviews I couldn't find elsewhere. People enjoyed what I wrote. They would e-mail me for advice or book suggestions for their children. Eventually I extended my reviews to appear as well on Epinions.com (a site similar to Amazon but that also pays). When I began a children's literary blog, it felt natural to copy the reviews I presented on Amazon onto my new site as well. And when the social book networking site Goodreads began, there was yet another place to put up reviews. Now, each personal review appears on three different websites online—Amazon, my blog, and Goodreads—reaching three different audiences in the process.

MOCK NEWBERY AND MOCK CALDECOTTS

A mock Newbery or mock Caldecott is a situation in which a group of people participate in a discussion of potential winners of the Newbery or Caldecott a month or two before the decisions are made by the official Newbery and Caldecott committees. Such committees are normally run for and by adults, though there are ways of conducting similar mock committees for kids too. The advantage of belonging to such a committee (whether it's a yearlong commitment or merely a month or two) is that you get exposure to books you may not have had much contact with before the experience. What's more, by discussing these books with other adults you get to determine each title's strengths and weaknesses. I've often found that discussions I've participated or listened in on at mock committees help me to talk up the books to children and their parents later. It's a quick way to get a sense of the committee process and offers people a chance to see what it's like to pick the "best" books

What's it like to run a mock Newbery?

I've done several mock Newberys with adults. I think doing it with kids is much more challenging, and I haven't tackled it. For a mock Newbery to work well—that is, for everyone to get a sense of the experience of the committee process—you need to have enough people for an effective discussion and vote, and everyone has to have read every title, which turns out to be nearly impossible. To get enough people (seven or nine is great), I think the key is to stick with it for a few years. I now have a core group. Having a blog so that people can easily find the date and book list is also helpful.

To get everyone to read all the titles, you have to make sure that you make a manageable reading list (eight to ten titles, not all heavy tomes), that most of the books are easy to locate in the fall (spring and summer titles will be available in the public library, but fall titles may not), and that you provide mechanisms for people to borrow the hard-to-locate copies. Then remind people over and over that the date is approaching and of the importance of reading the whole list.

Nina Lindsay, Oakland Public Library

in a group. And if you're serious about running such a group, you might want to consider purchasing Kathleen Simonetta, Nancy Hackett, and Linda Ward-Callaghan's excellent *Newbery and Caldecott Mock Elections* (2001). There's no better way to understand the process than by going straight to the professionals.

Some committees are formed immediately after the previous year's winner is announced. They then proceed to read all the books that they think have the potential to become winners. That's one way of doing it. Another way is to wait until the three months preceding the official announcement. Then a small group picks the potential winners (ten or so titles altogether). This list is disseminated, everyone reads the books, and then you gather to discuss and vote on the winners.

During the discussion of the candidates, it might be a good idea to follow a prescribed set of rules. Some mock committees enjoy a shortened version of the official Newbery/Caldecott committees. Each book is assigned to someone, who discusses it with the other members (who have also presumably read it). Each book is introduced and followed by a ten-minute or shorter discussion (the committee head will have to bang down the gavel to keep the discussion orderly). Finally, the first vote is taken. The numbers are tallied, and the winners can be determined one of two ways. You can follow the official Newbery/Caldecott rules and ask that everyone vote on their top four favorites. The top vote gets 5 points, the second gets 4, the third gets 3, and so on. There will then have to be a distinct point spread between the first winner and the runners-up. This may be an authentic way of conducting a mock committee, but depending on when you begin the discussion, it can also prove lengthy. If you begin your meeting at seven in the evening, you may be inclined to opt for a quicker method of selection. Consider the old "most votes wins" method.

Another too little lauded necessity is pizza and beverages. Anyone who has served on a professional committee will attest to the fact that a well-fed and well-watered committee is a happy committee.

These mock discussions can also be performed with children. The age of the participants depends on which award you would like them to participate in discussing. They will probably have to be older children, at least in terms of the Newbery, as the criteria state that Newbery books can be for any titles appropriate for children up to age fourteen. And as the book *Newbery and Caldecott Mock Elections* says, "Unless younger children already have a background in analyzing books, Newbery programs will be more rewarding for students in grades six and up" (Simonetta, Hackett, and Ward-Callaghan 2001, 19). Caldecott mock committees are perfect for younger children. All around the country, schools create these mock Caldecotts for their students, and libraries can do the same. If you have a book group, this can also be a theme for one of the meetings. You could also make a mock Caldecott into an after-school or weekend event for the public.

I attended my first mock Newbery/Caldecott while still in graduate school for my master's in library and information science. I didn't quite know what to expect but attended out of curiosity and a still yet undefined sense that I might want to serve on an official committee sometime in the future. In this case, the group had been sent a list of titles to seek out and read beforehand. Each title was discussed as a group, and at the end a quick vote was taken. Not counting the reading I did beforehand, the whole process couldn't have taken any longer than three hours. Consider creating something similar for your children's literary enthusiasts if you haven't a program like this in existence already.

Do you see any particular advantage to children's librarians blogging in some fashion? Is there a particular type of blogging they should consider engaging in?

The primary advantage: community.

As children's librarians, sometimes we are fortunate enough to work at a large location with other children's librarians where we can oooh and ahhh over the new picture books, share the "OMG" wonderful (or awful!) book that was just read, and bounce programming ideas off each other. More often than not, this is not the case, and even if one is involved in a local or statewide children's services group, those meetings are once a month at best. So how do you get to talk shop and share the things you love (or hate!) about being a children's librarian? Blogs, both by creating your own blog or by being an active commenter on other people's blogs.

There are other pluses, such as networking. Some librarians can get out of their branches for those monthly or bimonthly children's services meeting or go to ALA's conferences. Not everyone can do this. So how does the librarian who cannot leave the building or does not have funding get involved with the larger world of children's librarianship and children's literature? Blogs are an excellent way to meet and develop relationships with peers across the country and the world.

BLOGGING

And then there is the "B" word. Blogging is an occupation or hobby that proves easy to mock. Since anyone can blog, there is sometimes the assumption that everyone *does* blog. The user-friendly nature of the activity makes it appear to be some glorified form of journaling, one that any doofus with fingers and the Internet can participate in.

When blogging began to gain followers and enthusiasts, children's librarians were among the first fans of books for young people to take to this new skill. One of the first children's literary bloggers was Tasha Saedecker of the site Kids Lit (http://kidslit.menashalibrary.org). A *School Library Journal* article spread the word about people like Tasha, and before long an online community began to form. Composed of more than just librarians, the kidlitosphere lured in parents, booksellers, publishers, authors/illustrators, educators, professionals, and anyone with an interest in the field. A new award was created (the Cybils found at http://dadtalk.typepad.com/cybils/), and people began

Polishing writing skills is another positive benefit to blogging. A writer is their own editor for blogs. And whether it is sharing your thoughts on a recent news article about the state of children's literature, a review of a book, or a how-to guide to your latest cool program, blogging helps strengthen and develop writing skills.

Above all, blogging is fun! But it is also something that is personal. So what type of blogging really depends on what a person wants to talk about: New books? Old books? Programming? Outreach? Some blogs cover a wide range of topics, and others are very focused. There is always room for more blogs, especially by people who let their own distinct voice shine. Time can be a factor; blogging does take up time. When people say, "Where do you find the time?" my half-serious, half-joking answer is, "I don't knit"—meaning I don't have a hobby like knitting or scrapbooking; instead, I blog. If you think time may be a factor and that you cannot post as frequently as you see others do, comment! Commenting in blogs is just as big a contribution to the "blogosphere" as writing a blog. Group blogs are also a great way to reduce the "oh, no, it's been five days since I blogged, I must blog something" panic.

Elizabeth Burns, youth services librarian for an East Coast library for the disabled; coauthor of Pop Goes the Library *(2008); and contributor to the blog of the same name at www.popgoesthelibrary.com*

to organize "carnivals" of posts where a single person would aggregate a wide swath of postings.

Today the kidlitosphere has yearly meetings, organized book tours, and the ear of the industry. It can all prove a little daunting, and with so many blogs already in existence, what possible advantage would it be to add your voice to the pack?

First, when it comes to children's librarians, there aren't as many bloggers as you might think. When I blogged in New York City, I was the only librarian for quite some time, until eventually people from Queens and Manhattan joined. Even then, the maximum number of children's librarians I ever encountered in New York City who worked in the public library system and blogged was around four or five. Chances are that wherever you live, you may find one or two people interested in blogging, but for the most part librarians are such busy people that they don't often find time to blog as well as work.

Why do it? It comes down to what kind of blog you'd like to have. There are all kinds of ways to make use of the format. To my mind, there are three kinds of children's librarian blogs: the community blog, created with the sole purpose of speaking to the library's immediate patrons; the review blog, which tries to bring titles old and new to the attention of the masses; and the informational blog, which speaks to anything pertaining to the children's literary community. This kind of blog can contain huge swaths of ephemera and may prove to be more popular than the other kinds of blogs out there.

When I started as a children's librarian, I thought it might be a neat idea to create a blog for the children's room of my library branch. I would post information about traveling performers, storytimes, events, crafts, new books, and the community. Patrons who lived in the area would subscribe to the branch's RSS feed and get updates on the library, which would reinforce its importance to them. It didn't work out that way. I proposed the idea to the library system and was told that this was not an option. The problem back then was that we were in the early days of blogging. A site that would appear with the approval of the branch itself would require that the blog be edited, in a sense, so that the views and commentary that appeared meshed with the library's message. This was fine for the time and scope of the system I was working in, but smaller branches could easily do the same thing without the weight of red tape and problems. Perhaps you work in a small community and have a lot more leeway with new proposals like blogging. Suggest it to your library system, and if you get the go-ahead, go to it! Best of all, you'll be able to promote the books you love (both old and new) through your blog, potentially upping the library's circulation statistics.

Another kind of blog you might consider is the review-based blog. When my library system momentarily thwarted my attempt to blog, the solution to my problem was simple. If my library system didn't want me to represent their views, I could understand that. But why not represent my own instead? My blog, *A Fuse #8 Production,* began its life as a vehicle for the reviews I had been writing on Amazon.com for years. Every day I posted a new review of varying length, and the result was a new way to present my writing. At Amazon, I was a name without a face. Now my blog would declare my status as a children's librarian loud and proud, and I would be able to take some credit for my writing.

The review blog can be done in a variety of ways. Generally you want to provide information for patrons, parents, and fellow librarians. Including publication information, just as a professional review does, helps to specify whom the books are for. Your review length is entirely up to you and may depend on how much time you have in your day. The advantage of short reviews is that some people may not have time to scroll through your lengthy thoughts and ponderings on a title. Short reviews offer them bite-sized commentary, though it may prove harder to get a base if your writing isn't substantially different from that of other reviewers. It can be a good idea to offer additional information with your reviews as well. For example, you might want to include the author or illustrator's website, web videos, and book trailers pertaining to the title; links to professional reviews available for viewing online (newspapers are increasingly making this possible these days); and images from the book too. I also like to link to the reviews of fellow book reviewers, particularly those I've found to be the most interesting. For example, *The Well-Read Child* (http://wellreadchild.blogspot.com) frequently makes a point to include quotations from other bloggers' reviews on particularly salient points.

In terms of your immediate community, a review blog is a great way to make regular recommendations to your patrons. If someone asks you for a princess book for a five-year-old, you can update your blog to include the best princess stories out there. If someone else wants a list of recommendations, you can include it on your blog for easy printing. The review blog can develop a readership and, best of all, allow you to review titles that people might otherwise not hear about.

The third blog I call "informational," though the term may be too limiting considering the multiple purposes it serves. After I started posting reviews on my site, I found that a little filler sometimes helped a lot. I began to link to sites of particular interest to children's literary enthusiasts. News items, information for libraries, interviews with famous authors—I plucked anything that caught my interest from the blogosphere and presented it on my site with a link crediting the source. As children's literary blogs started to increase, I found it easier and easier to gather news items, and my readership began to rise in numbers. Other blogs have done similar postings, though they often concentrate in different areas. Some primarily interview the authors and illustrators who interest them the most. Others use their blogs as ways of writing funny pieces about picture books. Wherever your creativity and your interest takes you, that's your hook.

Of course, you may prefer to create a blog that is community, review, and informational all at once. However you prefer to do it, just remember that blogging is supposed to be fun. If you find that it's becoming just another aspect of your job that you want to put off or delay, don't bother with it. So far, few librarians have been required to blog on the job, though that may change as communities get their day-to-day information online more and more. Whatever you decide, blogging is a great way to supplement a job and have a bit of fun. Be sure to give it a try.

JOINING A PROFESSIONAL ORGANIZATION

For librarians, professional organizations offer support where you might otherwise flounder on your own. The degree to which you find this support useful depends greatly on your level of participation and the way in which the organization itself is run. From a professional standpoint, professional organizations can benefit librarians in ways that a mere presence online cannot.

Of the possible organizations you may wish to join, the American Library Association is undoubtedly the most powerful. Online it describes some of the potential benefits of joining as a way to "improve your visibility in the profession by participating in ALA, division, and round table committees and by writing or blogging for an ALA publication. ALA puts you in conversation with thousands of fellow members." It offers access to job opportunities and multiple library practices that you might not find elsewhere. And by joining, you can apply to be on a book committee like the Newbery, the Caldecott, the ALA Notables team, or any of the professional groups that determine the big awards for children's literature every year.

If you are a student, ALA offers student memberships at a cheaper rate. And from a monetary standpoint, your employer may be of use as well. Many public library systems reimburse their employees' yearly membership subscriptions or conference fees. Consider finding out if this is a possibility with your own employer rather than having to pay out of pocket. Or you may also wish to join a smaller division of ALA, like the Public Library Association. This is a group that seeks to "enhance the development and effectiveness of public library staff and services."

On a far more local level, you may wish to join your state library association. Sometimes membership with a smaller organization will offer the personal contact and interest that belonging to a larger organization like ALA lacks.

CONCLUSION

All of these activities, no matter how big or small, take up time—time you could be spending with your family, your garden, or your hobbies. I think it's important to remember that what I am advocating here is not that you do all these activities. I'm simply saying that a little care and attention spent, even as little as five minutes a day, on professional development outside the workplace can yield unexpected results. Your visit to a blog might lead you to discover the hot new series that a child asks you about the next day. A trip to a local children's bookshelf could alert you to local authors you never thought to highlight in your collection before.

You never know what may end up being useful.

My Favorite Middle-Grade Titles to Booktalk

The Sisters Grimm: The Fairy-Tale Detectives by Michael Buckley—Many kids have heard of this one by now, but if they haven't, it's a fun premise for a series. Two girls are taken in by a grandmother they've never heard of to live among fairy-tale characters who resent them. If the girls die, the characters are free to leave their small town. In the meantime, there are dirty dealings going on. Exciting stuff.

Phineas Gage: A Gruesome but True Story of Brain Science by John Fleischman—Any book that allows you to describe in detail a metal pole entering and exiting a man's brain but leaving the man fine (though a jerk) when it's over, *that's* good booktalk fodder.

The Black Book of Secrets by F. E. Higgins—What I love about booktalking this is that the first page is essentially a booktalk in and of itself. A boy wakes up strapped to a table where his parents are about to help a backroom "dentist" extract the kid's teeth for money. He escapes and joins with a man who collects secrets in a mysterious book. You can end the booktalk anywhere you like, but be sure to include those two details.

Savvy by Ingrid Law—Who doesn't want superpowers? This booktalk plays up the fact that Mibs is about to get her powers when she turns thirteen, but her father's accident changes everything and she finds herself with a power infinitely difficult to control. Be careful you don't give away what her power is. That's part of the lure.

The Mailbox by Audrey Shafer—When I booktalk this title,
I like to give just the initial premise. A boy comes
home and finds his uncle dead. He leaves, and when
he returns, the body is gone, and there's a letter in the
mailbox that simply says "I have a secret" on one side
and "Do not be afraid" on the other.

Eggs by Jerry Spinelli—Like *The Mailbox,* I like to end this
talk early in the book. Usually I talk about how the
main character finds a girl's body under a pile of
leaves during an Easter egg hunt. He leaves it there and
searches the newspapers for months to see if anyone
else found it, but no one ever has. Then one day he
sits in the back of the library as his grandmother does
a storytime and sees the girl sitting along the wall,
asleep. Sends a chill down their little spines, this
booktalk does.

Conclusion

There are some notions that don't bear dwelling on. Take the idea that you can't read every children's book ever published. In some small part of my brain, I don't want to believe that's true. I want to be able to live my life under the basic assumption that at some point, I will be "done" with all the great books written for youth. I'll close the back cover of the final book, place it resolutely on my desk, and rest easy. It's a pretty thought, but that's the thing about the children's publishing industry. We can never *be* done, and when you think about it, would you really want to be? Each year yields new treasures, new surprises, new titles that break through what we considered to be unbreakable boundaries. And as they pass through our hands and the hands of our young patrons, they become old books. If they are particularly good, they might even become classics. It is your intervention and attention that will help young readers remember such books. Your intervention that will turn these titles into beloved old friends.

How do children typically hear about new books? They hear about them from their teachers, television, friends, and local bookstore displays. How do teachers hear about new books? From marketing departments that directly contact them, online resources, and colleagues. How do parents hear about new books? From television shows, magazine articles, booksellers, and other parents—and, naturally, librarians. They all hear about great books from librarians like you and me. Librarians have an edge over the publishing industry. The sheer scope of materials under our fingertips, spanning time and market conditions, gives us the power to introduce masses of children to great books, old and new. We are the arbiters of great literature. There is still an understanding out there that says that librarians know how to seek out and promote great writing to the young.

If you can go forth and find a new way to get a youngster giddy about a work of children's literature, you are doing good work. Reaching that end means getting your hands dirty, though. You need to dive through your dusty, dirty stacks, read through them, and pluck out the treasures. You have to be willing to keep up with what's new and cool, separating the truly remarkably writing from the overmarketed, over-hyped dregs. You have to know and acknowledge our past, consider our future, and be conversant in discussing both. You have to polish up your performance skills, realizing that the librarian introvert is a rare and dying species. On top of all of this, you have to be willing to go the extra mile.

The great librarian Frances Clark Sayers once said, "I know that, in library school, students who know nothing about children's books come into my class to read children's books often with a little air of condescension. We must ourselves realize and convince others that books for children is a field which wants and demands and must demand the best efforts of creative artists and writers, men and women, whether they are writing for children or adults" (Jenkins 1996). And in this age where reading for pleasure is no longer the go-to youthful activity it might once have been, we librarians must also convince our young patrons that those best efforts we've located are worthy of their attention. Simply knowing what's out there is half the battle. Once you're confident in knowing your collection, you'll be able to convince others of its inherent worth. That's the beauty of the occupation.

Notable Children's Literary Awards

Batchelder Award—given to an American publisher for a children's book considered to be the most outstanding of those books originally published in a foreign language in a foreign country and subsequently translated into English and published in the United States.

Belpré Medal—honors a Latino/Latina writer and illustrator whose works best portray, affirm, and celebrate the Latino cultural experience in an outstanding work of literature for children and youth.

Caldecott Medal—honors the artist of the most distinguished American picture book for children.

Coretta Scott King Book Award—given to African American authors and illustrators for outstanding inspirational and educational contributions to promote understanding and appreciation of the culture of all peoples and their contribution to the realization of the American dream.

Cybils Award—Established in 2006 and given annually by the children's book blogger community in a variety of different categories and age ranges.

Geisel Medal—honors the author and illustrator of the most
    distinguished contribution to the body of American children's
    literature known as beginning reader books published in the
    United States during the preceding year.
Newbery Medal—honors the author of the most distinguished
    contribution to American literature for children.
Printz Award—an award for a book that exemplifies literary
    excellence in young adult literature.
Schneider Family Book Award—honors an author or illustrator for
    a book that embodies an artistic expression of the disability
    experience for child and adolescent audiences.
Sibert Informational Book Medal—honors the author and illustrator of
    the most distinguished informational book published during
    the preceding year.
Sydney Taylor Book Award—"Recognizes the best in Jewish children's
    literature. Medals are awarded annually for outstanding books
    that authentically portray the Jewish experience. The award
    was established in 1968."

Books with Great Recommended Lists of Children's Titles

Deeds, Sharon, and Catherine Chastain. 2001. *The new books kids like.* Chicago: American Library Association.

Freeman, Judy. 1990. *Books kids will sit still for.* New York: Bowker.

——. 1995. *More books kids will sit still for.* Westport, CT: Bowker-Greenwood.

Gebel, Doris. 2006. *Crossing boundaries with children's books.* Lanham, MD: Scarecrow Press.

Hearne, Betsy. 1999. *Choosing books for children: A commonsense guide.* Chicago: University of Illinois Press.

Odean, Kathleen. 2001. *Great books about things kids love: More than 750 recommended books for children 3 to 14.* New York: Ballantine Books.

Pearl, Nancy. 2006. *Book crush.* Seattle: Sasquatch Books.

Silvey, Anita. 2004. *100 best books for children.* Boston: Houghton Mifflin.

Stan, Susan. 2002. *The world through children's books.* Lanham, MD: Scarecrow Press.

Tomlinson, Carl M. 1998. *Children's books from other countries.* Lanham, MD: Scarecrow Press.

References

BOOKS

Anderson, Charles R., and Peter Sprenkle. 2006. *Reference librarianship: Notes from the trenches.* New York: Hawthorn Information Press.

Becker, May Lamberton. 1936. *First adventures in reading: Introducing children to books.* New York: Frederick A. Stokes Company.

Bishop, Kay, and Anthony Salveggi. 2001. Responding to developmental stages in reference service to children. *Public Libraries* 40:354–58.

Briggs, Diane. 1997. *52 programs for preschoolers: The librarian's year-round planner.* Chicago: American Library Association.

Broderick, Dorothy. 1977. *Library work with children.* New York: H. W. Wilson.

Burton, Melvin K. 1998. Reference interviews: Strategies for children. *North Carolina Libraries* 56:110–13.

Byatt, A. S. 2003. Harry Potter and the childish adult. *New York Times,* July 11.

Clark, Beverly Lyon. 2003. *Kiddie lit: The cultural construction of children's literature in America.* Baltimore, MD: Johns Hopkins University Press.

Cullinan, Bernice E., and Lee Galda. 2002. *Literature and the child,* 5th ed. Belmont, CA: Wadsworth/Thomson Learning.

Fletcher, William I. 1876. Public libraries and the young. In *Public libraries in the United States: Their history, condition, and management.* Washington, DC: Department of the Interior, Bureau of Education.

Freeman, Judy. 1990. *Books kids will sit still for.* New York: Bowker.

———. 1995. *More books kids will sit still for.* Westport, CT: Bowker-Greenwood.

Geller, Evelyn. 1984. *Forbidden books in American public libraries, 1876–1939: A study in cultural change.* Westport, CT: Greenwood Press.

Horning, K. T. 1997. *From cover to cover: Evaluating and reviewing children's books.* New York: HarperCollins.

Hunt, Clara Whitehall. 1917. Value in library work with children. In *Library work with children,* ed. Alice I. Hazeltine. New York: H. W. Wilson.

Jenkins, Christine A. 1996. Women of ALA Youth Services and professional jurisdiction: Of nightingales, Newberys, realism, and the right books 1937–1945. *Library Trends* 44:813–27.

Jennerich, Elaine Z., and Edward J. Jennerich. 1987. *The reference interview as a creative art.* Littleton, CO: Libraries Unlimited.

Langemack, Chapple. 2003. *The booktalker's bible: How to talk about the books you love to any audience.* Westport, CT: Libraries Unlimited.

MacDonald, Margaret Read. 1993. *The storyteller's start-up book: Finding, learning, performing, and using folktales.* Little Rock, AR: August House.

Marcus, Leonard. 2003. *Storied city: A children's book walking-tour guide to New York City.* New York: Dutton.

Moore, Anne Carroll. 1908. Library membership as a civic force. *Library Journal* 33 (7): 269–75.

Nelson, Sara. 2008. E-dreaming. *Publishers Weekly* 255, no. 26 (June 30).

Nesbitt, Helen. 1956. Books for children and young people. In *The nature and development of the library collection: With special reference to the small and medium-sized public library.* Papers presented at an institute conducted by the University of Illinois Library School, November 11–14, Graduate School of

Library Science. University of Illinois at Urbana-Champaign, Champaign, IL.

Nichols, Judy. 1987. *Storytimes for two-year-olds.* Chicago: American Library Association.

Oatman, Eric. 2005. NY Library says no to PG ratings. *School Library Journal,* July 1.

Pattee, Amy S. 2008. What do you know? Applying the K-W-L method to the reference transaction with children. *Children and Libraries* 6 (1): 30–39.

Riedling, Ann. 2005. *Reference skills for the school library media specialist: Tools and tips,* 2nd ed. Corinth, NY: Linwood Publishing.

Rollock, Barbara. 1988. *Public library services for children.* Hamden, CT: Library Professional Publications.

Salvadore, Maria. 2001. An interview with Virginia A. Walter, author of *Children and libraries: Getting it right. Journal of Youth Services in Libraries* 14 (3): 42–44.

Saricks, Joyce G., and Nancy Brown. 1997. *Readers' advisory service in the public library,* 2nd ed. Chicago: American Library Association.

Sayers, W. C. Berwick. 1932. *A manual of children's libraries.* London: Allen and Unwin.

Silvey, Anita. 2004. *100 best books for children.* Boston: Houghton Mifflin.

Simonetta, Kathleen, Nancy Hackett, and Linda Ward-Callaghan. 2001. *Newbery and Caldecott mock elections,* rev. ed. Chicago: American Library Association.

Smith, Duncan. 2001. Reinventing readers' advisory. In *The readers' advisor's companion,* ed. Kenneth D. Shearer and Robert Burgin. Englewood, CO: Libraries Unlimited.

Sullivan, Michael. 2005. *Fundamentals of children's services.* Chicago: American Library Association.

Tyack, D. B. 1978. Ways of seeing: An essay on the history of compulsory schooling. In *History, education, and public policy: Recovering the American educational past,* ed. D. R. Warren, 56–89. Berkeley, CA: McCutchan.

Walter, Virginia A. 2001. *Children and libraries: Getting it right.* Chicago: American Library Association.

Zipes, Jack (ed.), Lissa Paul, Lynne Vallone, Gillian Avery, and Peter Hunt. 2005. *The Norton anthology of children's literature.* New York: Norton.

WEB RESOURCES

ALA (American Library Association), www.ala.org/ala/ourassociation/
    membership/whyjoinala/index.cfm. Provides information and
    details about joining the American Library Association. ALA
    describes itself as "the place to be for the librarian or library
    worker with no spare time"—and for good reason.
PLA (Public Library Association), www.ala.org/ala/mgrps/divs/
    pla/index.cfm. According to its mission statement, PLA,
    which was created for public librarians, is "a member-driven
    organization that exists to provide a diverse program of
    communication, publication, advocacy, continuing education,
    and programming for its members and others interested in the
    advancement of public library service."

Index

You may also be interested in

Booktalking Bonanza: Transform your booktalks to engage your audience! With multimedia infusing nearly every activity, today's audiences from toddlers to elders expect lively, interactive presentations. Now two award-winning authors outline their kid-tested, proven models for enlivening traditional booktalks. Get up to speed with exciting media technologies like YouTube videos, online music, PowerPoint presentations, Internet resources, and audio and video from the library collection, along with food, games, puppets, and magic or science experiments.

Storytime Magic: Enriching and supplementing storytelling programs with fingerplays, flannelboards, and other props will be a cinch thanks to this generous sampling of art and craft ideas, songs, and action rhymes. This time-saving resource includes thematic organization to make program planning easy, recommended books for each theme, easy-to-follow craft and flannelboard patterns, and Quick Tips boxes that enhance the early literacy component.

The Newbery and Caldecott Awards, 2009 Edition: This indispensable annual guide covers the most distinguished American children's literature and illustration. Librarians and teachers everywhere have come to rely on it for quick reference, collection and curriculum development, and readers' advisory. With a fresh look and format, locating information on the award-winning books is easier than ever before.

More Family Storytimes: This book from best-selling author Rob Reid features stories, fingerplays, songs, and movement activities to enhance the time families spend at the library. Brimming with all new material, *More Family Storytimes* offers practical, creative, and active storytime programs that will captivate audiences of all ages.

For more information, please visit www.alastore.ala.org.